Price Guide to

American
COUNTRY
ANTIQUES

Fourth Edition

Don and Carol Raycraft

Photographers
George Bolster
Jim and Betty Clark
Bob and Judy Farling
Christopher Ryan Farling
Jo-Ann Heidenreich
Jean Ann Honegger
Carol Raycraft
Clay Kinchen Smith
Dennis White

On the cover: Cast iron windmill weight
made in Elgin, Illinois, c. 1880, $400-600.
Photograph by Carol Raycraft

Library of Congress Catalog
Card Number 770726
ISBN 0-87069-385-0

10 9 8 7 6 5 4 3 2 1

Published by

Wallace-Homestead Book Company
580 Water's Edge Road
Lombard, Illinois 60148

Acknowledgments

We would like to thank the following individuals and organizations for their assistance in putting this project together. Without their knowledge and friendship, the book could not have been written.

American Graniteware Association
Lois Balk
3 Behrs
Linda Buehrer
Jim and Betty Clark
Dr. David D. Darnall
Don and Linda Darst
Paula Davis
Shawn Dunston
Jon and Dianne Erpenbach
Bob and Judy Farling
Neal Ferguson
Frank and Berdean Freed
Betty Geoffroy
Bill Grande
Shelli Hall
Mary Hays
Tom Heldt

Gordon and Jean Ann Honegger
Dr. Alex Hood
Grant Hopkins
Joan Knodle
Phyllis Larson
C. B. Livingston
Jan McLain
D. A. Majors
Middle Tennessee Bottle Collectors Club
Gene Moore
Jim and Phyllis Ramsey
Scott Raycraft
David and Scott Schnitzer
George Schnitzer, Jr.
Janice Shores
Elizabeth Strickland
Gerry Sweem
Gloria Weiss

3

This book is dedicated to the memory of Linda Murray Dameron, whose friendship we shall always miss.

Contents

Introduction

Recently we talked with a southern Indiana friend about finding sources for antiques. The friend is a serious collector of American country antiques. By definition, a "serious collector" is one who…

- Can't remember his mother-in-law's name but knows the area and zip codes of most of the major dealers east of the Mississippi.
- Has anxiety attacks when remembering the decorated jug his spouse talked him out of at a show last summer.
- Is on a first-name basis with the loan officer at a minimum of three banks.
- Has a mail carrier who is suffering from a hernia caused by the delivery of last month's telephone bill.

Anyway, this collector had the following opinion about finding antiques.

"I really should be out there door-knocking. It's fun and frustrating at the same time. But when you find something nice and can buy it, it feels much like the old days. Bringing a good old grungy country piece home and cleaning it up after an afternoon in the country is an experience every antiquer should have. I think we rely too much on someone else these days to do the dirty work.

"I bought a red-and-black seven-foot cupboard two years ago from a Missouri dealer at an Ohio show who got it from a Michigan dealer who got it from a picker in southern Indiana who got it 15 miles from my front doorstep…knocking on doors!"

Now, in our section of Illinois, going door to door would probably result in the chance to buy an Avon collection, a debate about the relative merits of different seed corn varieties, a black eye, or a series of requests to vacate the premises as expeditiously as possible.

Therefore, while we appreciate our friend's enthusiasm for door-knocking, we find that most collectors limit their search to shows, markets, auctions, and traveling from shop to shop.

Shows

There is a current trend to reduce shows in length from three or four days to a single day or two. The concensus is that the expenses incurred by dealers at lengthy shows are not counterbalanced by increased sales.

There is also an interesting trend toward national shows. These are heavily promoted and attract dealers from all over the nation. Recently, successful shows were held in Tennessee, Texas, and Indiana following a great deal of nationwide publicity. Previously, most antiques shows were hyped regionally, and a majority of the dealers came from surrounding states.

At this point, it is premature to judge how long the national shows will be successful. As promoters attempt to lure collectors from wider geographic areas to their new shows, many cities may become oversaturated, and hosts and sales will suffer.

Outdoor Markets

There are numerous one-day outdoor markets in New England each summer, and other parts of the country hold their share, as well.

Most markets are held in large, open fields and last six to eight hours. The benefit of the market is that part-time dealers and collectors who don't go to shows often turn up with "fresh" merchandise.

Another advantage of markets is that the booth rental for dealers often is nominal, and dealers do not suffer the additional costs of days of food and lodging. The collector can see one hundred to five hundred dealers in one location without spending a week trying to catch many of them at home.

Antiques Shops

Historically, most collectors purchased antiques by driving from shop to shop. But rising costs, dwindling supplies of merchandise, and a changing market have forced many dealers to rent space in an antiques mall, which may have thirty to one hundred stalls. In such a mall, a dealer does not have to maintain regular hours, and his goods are constantly available for customers to see. An excellent example of this concept is the Lancaster Antiques Mall in Lancaster, Kentucky.

Price Guides

This book is designed to provide its readers with a "ball park" idea of the value of a particular American country antique. The estimates have been gathered through observation, discussion, and experience. We are collectors and have been for almost twenty years.

Prices change so rapidly that most price guides are probably dated before they arrive at the book store, and this volume is no exception. However, a price guide limited to a single field is often superior to a book that attempts to cover the entire antiques spectrum. As with all price guides, the reader must use this book only as a "guide" and not as a biblical work that is precise on every piece illustrated.

Trends

One of the major changes in the field of American country antiques in recent years is the growing power of the several early Americana magazines to shape the tastes of a huge buying public — a public that is strapped for original ideas.

At an outdoor show near York, Maine, in July of 1983, we had a discussion with a local dealer who described the incredible demand for birdhouses that developed after a pictorial article in *Country Living*. It reached the point where she was going from back yard to back yard trying to purchase birdhouses directly out of trees from amazed homeowners. One of her major dilemmas now is to guess which "antique" will be the next overnight sensation.

Records

There are American records for everything from cherry pitting to cow chip throwing. Listed below are some tentative all-time peaks for purchases of American antiques.

Basket: $3,520 for a double-tiered wall basket sold in 1982.

Chair table: $16,000 for an oval-top table with shoe feet from New England, c. eighteenth century.

Windsor chairs: $61,000 for a set of six brace-back chairs from Rhode Island, c. late eighteenth century.

Shaker furniture: $34,100 for a curly maple chest of drawers from Enfield, Connecticut, sold at auction in 1982.

Sled: $60,500 for a balsa wood prop sled marked "Rosebud" from the 1941 film "Citizen Kane." Sold in 1982.

Teddy bear: $1,045 for an early 15″ Steiff bear with button and shoebutton eyes sold in 1982.

Stoneware: $16,000 for a heart-shaped inkwell made by William Crolius, c. 1773.

Coverlet: $5,500 for a red, green, and rust-colored coverlet with a railroad decoration marked "Made by J. Lutz, E. Hempfield Township for Atty. Martin 1848." Sold in 1978.

Quilt: $16,000 for an appliquéd pictorial from the Ackerman family, Saddle River, New York, c. 1859. Sold in 1982.

Redware: $18,000 for a standing lion with yellow and brown glaze, made by the John Bell Pottery in the mid-nineteenth century. Sold in 1978.

A Less Publicized World Record

At the Brimfield, Massachusetts, outdoor market in the early summer of 1983, a major sale was of a stuffed chicken mounted on a post. We have paid as much as $7.95 for stuffed chicken, but we had it on a plate rather than on a post.

On a hot Sunday in July in Maine, we saw another stuffed chicken on a post for $125 (retail). This has to be approaching a world (or at least a new county) record.

Possibly a new county record for stuffed and mounted chickens.

1 Furniture

To be a successful collector of country furniture, you should buy intellectually, not emotionally. Don't become overwhelmed by the first appealing piece you see. Instead, inspect the piece thoroughly to make sure it is what it appears to be.

Paint

It is crucial to understand the difference between "original" paint and "early" paint. Original paint was the first coat. Any coat that followed and is seventy-five to one hundred fifty years old can be described as "early." "Late" paint may be three days, three years, or thirty years old.

With the demand for painted country furniture steadily rising, it is not unusual to find an old cupboard or pie safe with a new coating of color. To increase a piece's value, some dealers "move around" the old paint. This is done by using paint remover or stripper to loosen the old paint, then recoating the piece with its original paint.

The most sought-after colors for painted furniture are blue, yellow (ocher) or mustard, red, green, and bittersweet (a cross between red and orange).

Wood

Most nineteenth-century country furniture, such as cupboards, dry sinks, or benches, was made from pine and painted. Maple was used for beds and in combination with several other woods for chairs. The plank seats of most country chairs were pine, and the spindles were usually hickory. Maple was useful for legs, stretchers, and crest rails.

Occasionally, walnut was used for country cupboards and chests. Unlike the softer woods of poplar and pine, walnut furniture was not often painted.

Construction

Before purchasing any piece of country furniture, carefully check all aspects of its construction. Inspect chair and table legs to see if they have been "pieced out" (a section added to the bottom of each leg for additional height). And check the bottoms and backs of cupboards or dry sinks to detect replacement parts or dry rot.

Cupboards with solid doors (blind-front) often lose their doors and are turned into more desirable open cupboards. A careful check should detect traces of the hinges that held the original doors.

Getting the Best Deal

It has been our experience that the best time to purchase a large cupboard, chest, or desk is in the closing moments of the last day of an antiques show. Many dealers don't look forward to carting a large piece of furniture down the road and often are eager to sell it at a discounted price after sharing a booth with it for two or three days.

Before you pay a large sum for a piece of furniture, find out what you can about its history. However, keep in mind that most dealers can only trace a piece back to the dealer or private party from whom they purchased it. Many times a piece has passed through so many hands that even the lies about where it originally came from are confused.

Painted pine storage boxes
"As found" condition, New England, sides nailed rather than dovetailed, c. late nineteenth century.   *$75-95 each*

Painted pine dry sink
Original paint, New England, probably c. mid-nineteenth century.   *$600-850*

Comb-decorated blanket box
New England, c. 1830.   *$600-850*

Pine immigrant's trunk
Reinforced sides, dovetailed construction. Probably Scandinavian in origin, c. mid-nineteenth century.   *$375-575*

Carpenter's storage trunk
Pine, never painted, dovetailed construction, c. 1880-1900.   *$250-350*

Decorated storage boxes
New England, c. 1820-1840. ***$275-400*** *each*

Decorated storage boxes
New England, c. 1820-1835. The decoration on these boxes was done with a sponge dipped in thinned paint. ***$300-400*** *each*

Six-board pine chest
Cotter pin hinges, painted red. New England, dated "1826" on the back. ***$500-600***

Six-board pine blanket box
Bootjack ends, painted, c. late eighteenth century. Boldly painted on the back of this storage box is "1798." The construction techniques used and the cotter pin hinges suggest that the date could be accurate. ***$600-750***

11

Six-board blanket or storage box
Bootjack ends, red paint, c. 1840-1850.
$425-525

Blanket box
Bracket base, painted, pine, New England, c. 1850.
$450-500

Sugar chest
Pine, painted, probably from Kentucky or Tennessee, mid-nineteenth century. **$475-600**

Pine dry sink
Refinished, c. mid-nineteenth century.
$550-650

Bucket bench—dry sink
Pine, painted, c. mid-nineteenth century.
$600-800

Painted dry sink
Pine, probably from eastern Ohio or Pennsylvania, c. mid-nineteenth century. **$850-1,150**

Unusually well-built dry sink
Walnut, turned drawer pulls, c. 1860.
$1,200-1,400

Painted dry sink
Bootjack ends, pine, c. 1840-1860. This is an early form of dry sink. The addition of doors under the well or trough would make it a conventional sink. **$575-775**

Pine dry sink
Painted, probably from Pennsylvania or Ohio, c. 1860-1875. **$950-1,300**

Pie safe
Poplar, "as found" condition, factory-made, c. 1870-1900. A piece of furniture that is described "as found" is in the same condition as the day it was pulled from a barn loft, attic, or basement. Pie safes do not age gracefully if exposed to moisture and high humidity. The tins are highly susceptible to rust and can rapidly deteriorate.   **$450-550**

Painted dry sink
Measures 30" wide, c. mid-nineteenth century.
                                                    $575-700

Pine pie safe
Sixteen hand-pierced tins, probably from Pennsylvania, painted blue, c. 1850-1870. The tins allowed air to circulate within the cabinet and kept insects and rodents out. The factory-produced safes have tins that were stamped rather than individually hand-punched with a sharp nail.   **$1,100-1,400**

Pine pie safe
Pennsylvania, painted, c. 1850.   **$650-750**

Hand-pierced tin in pine pie safe

Drawer in the bottom of the pie safe
Most pie safes have a drawer in the top rather than bottom.

Pie safe
Pine, painted, "as found" condition, Midwestern, c. 1880. This pie safe has no major structural problems, but the paint has reached the point where it will have to be removed. The tins are gone and screen wire has been used as a replacement. A major factor in evaluating a safe is the uniqueness and condition of the pierced tin inserts.   **$150-225**

Pine corner cupboard
Uncommonly found size, probably from Kentucky, c. 1830-1840. **$1,200-1,500**

Step-back cupboard
Blind-front, painted pine, c. 1830-1850.
$850-1,100

Step-back open cupboard
Pine, painted red, southern Indiana, c. mid-nineteenth century. **$1,300-1,600**

16

Blind-front cupboard
Poplar and pine, probably from Ohio, c. 1840. **$900-1,100**

Painted pine cupboard
*Step-back, two-piece, Ohio, c. mid-nineteenth
century. Cupboards were often constructed in
two pieces or sections so they could be
transported easily in a horse-drawn wagon
when the family moved.* **$1,000-1,300**

Blind-front cupboard
Painted, pine, c. mid-nineteenth century.
$700-900

Miniature step-back cupboard
*Open-front, painted pine, c. mid-nineteenth
century.* **$700-950**

17

Open-front cupboard

Painted pine, step-back construction, c. 1840. This type of cupboard should be closely checked to see if it has been converted from a blind front with doors to an open front. The bottom of the cupboard should also be examined to see if it has been cut down because of dry rot. **$1,200-1,500**

Painted pine press or storage cupboard
New England, c. mid-nineteenth century.
$750-950

Chimney cupboard
Pine, painted, New England, c. 1850.
$850-1,000

Pine open cupboard
Painted, c. 1830-1845.   **$1,200-1,400**

Blind-front, step-back cupboard
Pine, painted, New England, c. 1840.
                     $1,400-2,000

Jelly or kitchen storage cupboard
Painted pine, c. 1870. The color of a cupboard can double its worth. If the paint is an especially attractive shade of blue or yellow, the value could be tripled.   **$500-750**

Two-piece pine cupboard
Blind-front, step-back, painted, c. mid-nineteenth century. **$1,200-1,600**

Pine open cupboard
Step-back, painted, c. 1820-1840.
$1,500-2,000

Pine cupboard from Indiana
Paneled doors, red and dark green paint, c. 1850. **$1,500-2,000**

Uncommon apothecary cupboard
Possibly from a physician's office, New England, c. 1840. **$2,200-2,800**

Pine cupboard
Blind-front, painted, c. mid-nineteenth century. **$700-1,000**

Pine wardrobe or storage cupboard
Uncommon size, painted pine, c. 1870.
$1,000-1,400

21

Jelly or storage cupboard
Pine, refinished, c. 1870.   ***$350-450***

Jelly or storage cupboard
Pine, refinished, c. 1850.   ***$400-500***

Factory-made kitchen cupboard
Pine, original varnished finish, c. 1900-1915. At $500, these mass-produced cupboards are incredibly overpriced. The early examples were made of pine or poplar and are relatively simple. The later oak versions with etched glass rather than wooden doors are in even greater demand.   ***$500-600***

Pine cupboard or dish dresser
Refinished, c. 1870.   **$700-775**

Storage cupboard
Pine, painted, c. mid-nineteenth century.
$800-1,200

Chimney cupboard
Painted, pine, hand-wrought iron hinges with rosehead nails, c. late eighteenth to early nineteenth century. This might have been built into a brick wall near the hearth to keep food warm. Chimney cupboards were designed to catch the radiated heat from the fire. A built-in can also be called an architectural piece.
$600-800

23

Early pine storage cupboard
H hinges with rosehead nails, eighteenth century.   **$575-700**

Pine chimney cupboard
Painted, c. 1840-1860.   **$375-450**

Apothecary chest
Pine, refinished, New England, replaced drawer pulls, c. mid-nineteenth century.
                                    $1,200-1,400

Apothecary chest
Painted pine, c. 1830-1850.   **$1,500-2,000**

Storage bin from an Indiana country store
Lift lids, pine, c. 1880. **$700-1,200**

Nut-and-bolt cabinet
Factory-made, oak, stenciled size markings on the drawer fronts, c. 1870-1915. **$850-1,100**

Meal or grain bin
Pine, painted, c. late nineteenth to early twentieth century. **$250-325**

Meal or grain bin
Pine, painted, c. late nineteenth to early twentieth century. **$200-225**

25

Unusual combination of drawers and storage bins
Painted a robin's egg blue, probably needs refinishing, "as found" condition, structurally sound, c. late nineteenth century. **$750-950**

Coffee bin
Pine, stenciled brand name, c. late nineteenth century. The quality of the stenciled product name is the primary factor in evaluating a wooden coffee bin. **$350-375**

Lamp or bedside table
Pine, refinished, c. 1850-1860. **$225-275**

Pine storage bin for firewood
Painted, c. 1900. **$300-375**

Lamp or bedside table
Painted, pine, c. mid-nineteenth century.
$300-350

Tavern table
Pine, two-board top, painted, c. 1840.
$450-575

Washstand
Finish grained to resemble oak, factory-made,
c. 1870. **$275-400**

Kitchen table
Maple base and legs, pine top, factory-made,
c. 1860. **$400-525**

Tavern table
Pine, painted base and scrubbed top, c. mid-nineteenth century. **$450-475**

Sideboard serving table
Walnut, from Kentucky or Tennessee, c. mid-nineteenth century. **$550-725**

Cricket table
Painted base and scrubbed top, c. 1860-1880. **$475-600**

Sawbuck table
Pine, c. early nineteenth century. **$525-675**

Sawbuck table
Pine, painted base and scrubbed top, c. early
nineteenth century.   *$600-850*

Dropleaf dining table
Tapered legs, maple, painted red with
scrubbed top, c. 1830-1850.   *$650-800*

Farm food preparation or "work" table
Maple and pine, c. 1870.   *$500-750*

Kitchen table
Maple base and pine top, c. mid-nineteenth
century.   *$600-850*

Hutch table
Red base, scrubbed top, New England,
nineteenth century.   *$1,400-1,800*

29

Pine desk
Painted blue, lift lid, c. 1870. **$800-1,100**

Dropleaf dining table
Maple and pine, c. 1830-1850. **$600-800**

Dough box
Pine, splayed sides, turned legs, c. 1840-1860. **$525-725**

Storage cupboard
Uncommon style, painted red, pine, c. 1840-1860. **$675-800**

Low post, rope bed
Pine and maple, painted red, c. mid-nineteenth century. **$600-750**

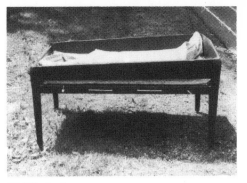

Child's bed
Uncommon style, painted pine and maple, rope supports, c. 1860. **$350-550**

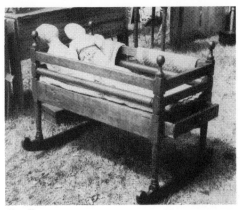

Cradle
Maple, painted, c. late nineteenth century. This is one of the few cradles we have ever seen that has a drawer. **$485-600**

Low post bed
Pine and maple, painted, rope supports, c. 1850. **$625-800**

Trundle bed
Pine and maple, rope supports, painted, c. 1840. **$400-500**

Early factory-made chest of drawers
Bun feet, pine, c. mid-nineteenth century. **$475-600**

Chest of drawers
Pine, painted, original drawer pulls, decorative apron, c. 1825-1845. **$800-1,000**

Shoemaker's or cobbler's bench
Pine with maple legs, c. first half of the nineteenth century. **$625-800**

Another view of the cobbler's bench
Note how the legs were mortised through the pine plank seat.

Cobbler's bench
Pine, c. mid-nineteenth century. **$600-700**

Cobbler's bench
Stand-up type, pine, painted, pin construction and dovetailed drawers, New York State, c. 1830. **$900-1,100**

Drying rack for dishes
Pine case with hickory dividing rods, New England, c. 1850. **$275-350**

32

Bucket bench

Pine, painted, nineteenth century. Bucket benches are difficult to date because they were used daily and because their form changed little in almost a century. The earlier versions were constructed more carefully, with mortised rather than nailed or braced joints.

$250-300

Set of steps

Also used as a plant stand, pine, painted, early twentieth century. $95-120

Bucket bench

Uncommon size, possibly from Pennsylvania, painted, pine, nineteenth century. $330-400

Spinning wheel

Southeastern United States, nineteenth century. Spinning wheels have limited marketability because of their unwieldy size. They take up a great deal of space in most contemporary homes and can serve no useful purpose.

$300-375

33

Slat- or ladder-back rocking chair
*Splint seat, painted, maple, c. mid-nineteenth
century.* **$175-250**

Slat- or ladder-back child's rocking chair
*Caned rattan seat, maple, painted, c. 1860-
1870.* **$140-175**

Slat- or ladder-back rocking chair
Maple, painted, c. mid-nineteenth century.
$275-375

Footstool
*Maple, designed for a taped footrest, nine-
teenth century.* **$65-75**

"Log" rocking chair
Designed to be used on a porch, similar in
style to "rustic" furniture designed for use in
summer homes in late nineteenth century.
$225-250

Boston rocking chair
Scrolled seat, stenciled decoration, often described as a lyre-back or fiddle-back, c. 1860-
1875. $350-400

Slat- or ladder-back child's highchair
New England, maple, painted, c. 1820-
1835. $600-800

Slat- or ladder-back rocking chair
Painted, maple, c. 1880. $160-185

Children's armchairs
Replaced splint seats, painted, maple and pine, c. early nineteenth century.
$275-350 *each*

Rod-back child's highchair
Splayed legs, painted, c. mid-nineteenth century. **$145-175**

Step-back cupboard
Open or dish dresser style, pine, painted, c. first half of the nineteenth century.
$1,600-2,000

36

Rod-back child's highchair
Maple, painted, c. mid-nineteenth century.
$175-210

Child's potty chair
Pine, painted, c. late nineteenth century.
$65-85

Set of four loop-back Windsor side chairs
Pine seats and maple legs, New England,
c. 1840.   **$1,000-1,200** set

Slat-back chairs
Rush seats, stenciled crest rails, maple,
c. 1860-1870.   **$500-650** set of four

37

Birdcage Windsor chairs
Pine seats, bamboo turnings, New England,
c. 1800-1830. **$385-550** *each*

Rod-back armchair
Splayed legs, bamboo turnings, New England,
c. 1800-1840. **$575-800**

Slat- or ladder-back chairs
Splint seats, uncommon number of slats,
painted, maple, c. 1830. **$300-375** *each*

Half spindle-back chairs
Pine plank seats, painted, originally stenciled,
made in early chair factory, c. mid-nineteenth
century. **$700-800** *for five chairs*

Slat- or ladder-back armchair
Splint seat, great turnings, New England, maple, painted, c. early nineteenth century.
$725-900

Slat- or ladder-back armchair
Painted, originally from Pennsylvania, c. late eighteenth century or early nineteenth century. **$800-1,200**

Spindle-back side chairs
Painted and stenciled, factory-made, c. mid-nineteenth century. **$100-135 each**

39

Comb-back side chairs
Painted, New England, splayed leg construction, pine seats, c. late eighteenth century to early nineteenth century.

$2,200-2,800 set of four

Chippendale-style side chair
New England, rush seat, black paint, c. late eighteenth century. $950-1,200

Sheraton-style Windsor settee or settle
Mustard paint, 72" long, c. 1820.

$2,500-3,000

Settle bench
Walnut, uncommon style, c. 1830.

$900-1,200

Comb-back Windsor chair
New England, great turnings, maple, painted, splayed legs, c. late eighteenth century.
$1,200-1,400

Refinished rocking chair
Splint seat, c. late nineteenth century. **$75-85**

Wagon seat or bench
Splint seat, maple, painted, c. early nineteenth century. The wagon seat or bench could be used in a horse-drawn wagon or taken into a church, meeting place, or home. **$675-900**

2 Kitchen Antiques

In this book, we've included information on two types of country kitchen antiques — woodenware and graniteware.

Woodenware

Though it may be hard to believe, Shaker boxes, heavily decorated stoneware, and painted dry sinks are considerably easier to find than handcrafted wooden kitchen implements made in the United States prior to 1850.

Early woodenware, such as spoons, noggins (pitchers), and trenchers (plates), were used daily. When cracked or chipped beyond simple repair, they immediately went into the fire as kindling. Early woodenware gradually ceased to exist because it was replaced by stoneware, pewter, and china and because, after 1850, much of the American woodenware was mass-produced in factories.

In recent years, a great influx of imported wooden and iron, kitchen-related "antiques" have been offered for sale by mail order. These pieces are generally crudely done, inexpensive in comparison to American antiques, and are purchased by collectors who don't realize what they are buying.

Materials Used in Woodenware

Maple was selected for most kitchen implements. It was plentiful, smooth, and durable. It also did not retain the odors of various foods or liquids with which it came in contact.

Pine was often used for covers to boxes, firkins (sugar buckets), and barrels because it was light in weight, seldom retained odors, and was watertight.

Hickory was often selected for the hoops or bands that held together staved buckets, barrels, and churns.

Burl, a knot or wart that protrudes from several varieties of trees, was used in making a variety of almost indestructible wooden bowls, plates, and mortars and pestles. Today, burl bowls are especially valuable.

Burls used for woodenware usually came from maple or ash trees. After the burl was cut from the tree, the bark was removed. Then the crafter started a fire on the flat side of the burl and allowed it to burn until charcoal formed. At this point, the craftsman put out the fire and hollowed out the charred portion to make the woodenware piece. Burl woodenware is especially strong because it has no regular graining pattern and, therefore, is less susceptible to cracking.

Techniques of Manufacturing Woodenware

The use of a lathe in the production of kitchenware is not a nineteenth-century development. Some variation of the lathe was used in Europe more than eight hundred years ago to turn out bowls, poles, and plates.

Butter prints and molds were usually shaped on a lathe and then steamed to soften the wood. When the wood was pliable, a design was impressed into the wood. The designs on early prints and molds were drawn in pencil on the flat pine or maple surface and were then carefully carved out with a draw knife or chip-carved with a chisel.

If a piece of woodenware was handcrafted rather than machine made, it should carry some telltale mark of a knife, chisel, or human error. Because machines don't make mistakes, pieces produced in a factory will not carry any hints of individual techniques.

Signs of Heavy Use

Kitchen antiques that were used on a daily basis should show some signs of wear. For instance, daily contact with milk or cheese leaves an odor in the bottom of a bucket that cannot be removed. Dairy products bleach pine or maple in exactly the same fashion as soap, giving woodenware the same patina as a pine tabletop that has been scrubbed down after each evening meal for twenty years. So, if the wooden kitchen antique came into contact with butter, cheese, milk, or soap, its surface should have been whitened or bleached.

Alice Morse Earle's *Home Life in Colonial America* (Berkshire Traveler Press), originally published in the late nineteenth century, is an invaluable resource for learning how kitchen articles were used on a daily basis.

Availability of American Woodenware

Commonly Found

For the most part, all of the items listed below were factory-made in huge quantities. The majority date from after 1880. Please note that "commonly found" does not necessarily mean "cheaply found."

pantry boxes
turned round bowls
staved butter churns with wire bands
butter paddles or workers
butter prints and molds
round breadboards
sugar buckets with metal bands
clothespins
lemon squeezers
meat pounders
potato mashers
pie lifters
rolling pins
sausage guns
washboards or scrub boards
wooden washing machines
root bowls labeled "burl"
spice boxes
papier-mâché funnels
papier-mâché bowls
chopping knives
sap buckets

Uncommonly Found

These items are a little more difficult to find and require a larger financial outlay. An attempt should be made to acquire them in

their original form rather than after restoration or refinishing.

pie peels
hearth brooms
canteens
cheese boxes (with buttonhole hoops)
mortars and pestles
wooden funnels
scrubbing sticks
Shaker oval boxes with "lappers"
    or fingers
maple sugar molds
cookie prints
cookie rollers
pie crimpers
hand-carved butter prints and molds
pantry boxes in great paint
butter churns with wooden bands
painted handcrafted spice chests
    ("box of drawers")
wooden apple parers
cheese ladders
butter scales

Rarely Found

It almost takes death or divorce to bring the items below back into the marketplace from long-established private collections.

trenchers (plates)
keelers (shallow tubs used to cool milk)
noggins (pitchers made from single blocks
    of wood)
burl bowls
burl mortars and pestles
smoothing boards
toddy sticks
piggins (open buckets with an extended
    handle)
wooden tankards
turned sugar bowls
cheese drainers
dish drainers

Butter Prints and Molds

The primary factor in determining the value of a butter print or mold is the design that has been carved or mechanically impressed into the wood. There are numerous varieties of each of the designs listed below.

Commonly Found

pine twigs	simple leaves
ferns	geometric designs
snowflakes	stars
concentric circles	rosettes

Uncommonly Found

swans	pineapples
acorns	grapes
sheafs of wheat	initials
sunflowers	flowers
strawberries	

Rarely Found

hearts	fish
roses	roosters
American eagles	rabbits
cows	birds
tulips	flying ducks
sheep	words or phrases

Hand-carved pineapple butter print.

Sheaf of wheat, found in many variations.

Commonly found four-leaf butter print.

Rare butter print of bird.

Very rare American eagle butter print.

Chip-carved heart butter print.

Stack of sugar buckets
Factory-made, c. late nineteenth century.
$110-145 *each*
$585-650 *stack of four*

Sugar bucket or firkin
Staved construction, bail handle, painted, factory-made, c. late nineteenth century. Sugar buckets were mass-produced well into the twentieth century. They were usually primarily of pine, though the mid-nineteenth century versions sometimes had hickory or ash hoops. They can also be found with metal or wire bands. Wooden handles are thought to be earlier than the wire bail with a maple grip.

Color is a critical factor in determining the worth of a sugar bucket. Blue is the most valuable, followed by yellow, mustard, red, bittersweet, or green. White is probably the least desirable color. **$110-145**

Stack of sugar buckets

Factory-made, c. late nineteenth century. The second bucket in the stack has a wire bail handle with a maple grip. The bottom two buckets have "fingers" or "lappers" nailed to the pine staves with copper or iron nails. Generally these are labeled Shaker and sold for considerably more than their actual value. Several of the New England Shaker communities did make sugar and syrup buckets and sold them to the "world." Many of these buckets have the name of the particular Shaker group and the location of the community impressed into the bottom of the bucket.

$110-145

Mincemeat firkin

Factory-made, painted with original "Atmore Mince Meat" label, c. late nineteenth century. The label adds a minimum of $15-35 to the value of this bucket. Note the stapled "finger" on the staved bucket. The staple dates the piece from the 1880-1915 period. **$145-160**

47

Painted sugar buckets
Wooden bail handles, painted, c. late
nineteenth century.   **$110-145**

Pantry boxes
Factory-made, painted, c. 1870 to the early
twentieth century. In the early 1970s, pantry
boxes were often hidden in the back of shops
and sold for $10-20 each. But when a photo-
graph in Early American Life showed a
kitchen in an Ohio home with a pine cupboard
filled with painted pantry boxes in a rainbow
of colors, the demand for and price of the
boxes increased dramatically. The color of a
box is now a primary determinant of value.
                                       $60-110

Pantry boxes
Factory-made, ranging in size from 4" to 15"
in diameter, c. late nineteenth to early twen-
tieth century.
Painted boxes: **$50-75**
Pantry box with bail handle: **$85-125**
Pantry box, unpainted, 15" in diameter:
                                       $65-75

48

Collection of nineteenth-century miniature buckets, pantry boxes, firkins, and bail-handle pantry boxes.

Unusual bail-handle bucket
Pine, staved construction, painted, twisted hickory hoops, c. mid-nineteenth century.
$150-185

Nest of three painted pantry boxes
Late nineteenth century. Woodenware companies did make pantry boxes in nests or stacks of four to eight. They were used for general storage of dry foodstuffs and kitchen materials. Few complete nests or even partial nests have survived because boxes were thrown out when they cracked or a lid was misplaced. This nest is missing some of the boxes that would stack between the smallest (4" in diameter) and the largest (14" in diameter).
Nest of three painted boxes: **$250-300**

Lathe-turned maple bowl
Painted, 11" in diameter, c. 1870-1890. Color is important in determining the value of these bowls. If a bowl is painted an exceptional shade of blue, its value could easily be doubled or tripled. **$70-95**

Maple work or dough bowl
Hand-hewn, painted, c. mid-nineteenth century. **$450-550**

Lathe-turned maple bowl
Painted white, c. late nineteenth century. **$55-70**

Pantry boxes
Ranging from 5" to 18" in diameter c. late nineteenth century.
Nest of four boxes in similar colors:**$375-450**
Painted, 18"-diameter pantry box: **$135-155**

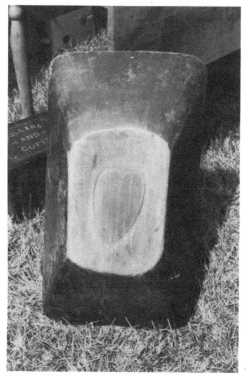

Bottom of the work bowl
A heart-shaped patch was used to cover an area worn through from heavy use. This patch makes a good bowl a great bowl.

Factory-made breadboard
Maple, original finish, "Bread" impressed by machine, c. late nineteenth to early twentieth century. Mail order houses sold thousands of these with matching knives from 1890-1920. The more elaborate the impressed "Give Us This Day," the more valuable the board.
$45-60

Pine, maple, and walnut chopping board
Probably early twentieth century. Cutting boards suffer so much daily use that they age prematurely. This makes the handmade boards almost impossible to date. Many produced by Boy Scouts for Christmas presents to their mothers in 1952 are probably labeled nineteenth-century today.
Pine and maple boards: **$40-65** each
Walnut board: **$65-75**

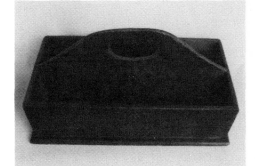

Knife and fork box
Maple, refinished, c. late nineteenth century. **$55-70**

Knife and fork box
Painted pine, c. mid-nineteenth century. **$85-95**

Knife sharpening or scouring box
Pine and maple, refinished, c. late nineteenth century.   **$50-60**

Wall box
Used for storage, painted red, pine, rosehead nails, c. late eighteenth to early nineteenth century.   **$350-475**

Knife sharpening or scouring box
Maple, c. nineteenth century.   **$60-70**

Wall box
Pine, painted, lift lid, c. late eighteenth to early nineteenth century.   **$350-450**

Candle box
Pine, refinished, c. early nineteenth century. **$150-225**

Butter workers
Maple, roughed out on a machine and then finished by hand, c. late nineteenth century. Fifteen years ago, these were plentiful and sold for $4-8 each. They were not used to scoop butter, but to work the water out of freshly churned butter. **$28-40** each

Candle box
Pine, painted, slide top, c. early nineteenth century. **$175-240**

Wooden flour or sugar scoops
Maple, refinished, c. late nineteenth century.
Large scoop: **$90-125**
Small scoop: **$85-100**

Flour or sugar scoop
Refinished, made from a single piece of maple, c. late nineteenth century. These can be found in a wide variety of sizes. The best examples are always made from a single piece of maple. **$90-125**

Dough box
Pine, painted, New England, c. 1840-1860. This dough box or trough is elaborately constructed with a handle on the lid and extensions on both ends for carrying the box. **$225-275**

Miniature chest
Handcrafted, pine, painted, spools for drawer pulls, c. mid- to late nineteenth century.
$135-150

Dough box
Pine, painted, c. mid-nineteenth century.
$175-225

Cranberry scoop
New England, c. early twentieth century.
$130-145

Miniature storage chest
Probably used for nuts, bolts, nails; glass drawer pulls; c. nineteenth century. **$185-225**

Hanging wall box
Used for storage, painted, pine, c. 1830-1840. **$145-175**

Spoon rack
Grained pine, nineteenth century. **$240-300**

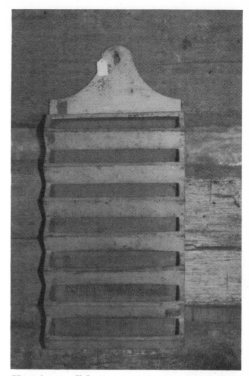

Storage box
Scandinavian in origin, painted, pine, c. mid-nineteenth century. **$300-350**

Butter churn
Made from a single piece of maple, uncommon style, original dasher and lid, not painted, c. first half of the nineteenth century. **$285-385**

Barrel butter churn
Sawbuck holder, staved construction, c. 1870. **$245-300**

Barrel butter churn
Staved construction, iron bands, c. 1870.
$175-215

Cake board
Hand-carved, walnut, 28" x 16", New York
State, c. 1820-1835. **$500-600**

Two-pound butter mold
Uncommon style, maple, c. late nineteenth
century. **$165-185**

One-pound butter mold
Dovetailed case, maple, nineteenth century.
$85-100

Cow butter mold
Maple, nineteenth century. **$245-275**

Carved butter print
"Lollipop" form, pine, refinished, different design on each side, c. early nineteenth century. **$250-300**

Two-pound box butter mold
Dovetailed case, maple, nineteenth century. **$125-145**

Butter mold
Elk design, probably from Maine, nineteenth century. **$850-950**

Intricately carved heart print
C. mid-nineteenth century. **$235-250**

Box mold
Four-leaf design, mid-nineteenth century.
$125-140

Butter print
Almost 4" in diameter, sheaf of wheat design, c. late nineteenth century. **$85-95**

Turkey butter print
Four inches in diameter, c. mid-nineteenth century. **$525-550**

Variety of butter mold forms
Factory-produced, c. late nineteenth century.

Half-moon butter stamp
Rare American eagle design, c. mid-nineteenth century. **$550-575**

Strawberry print
Maple, c. late nineteenth century. **$75-90**

Snowflake print
C. late nineteenth century. **$100-135**

Swan print
Maple, c. late nineteenth century. **$150-175**

Flower and leaf print
Maple, c. late nineteenth century. **$65-80**

Pineapple plant print
C. late nineteenth century. **$95-115**

Four-leaf print
Pine, hand-carved, c. mid-nineteenth century. **$100-115**

Pineapple butter print
Maple, c. mid-nineteenth century. **$175-195**

Eight-star print
C. mid-nineteenth century. **$145-160**

Sheaf of wheat print
Maple, c. late nineteenth century. **$75-95**

Strawberry print
Maple, c. mid-nineteenth century. **$160-175**

Double sheaf of wheat
C. late nineteenth century. **$75-95**

Sunflower print
Maple, c. mid-nineteenth century. **$115-140**

Cow butter print
Maple, c. mid- to late nineteenth century.
$275-300

Strawberry print
Maple, c. late nineteenth century. **$110-120**

Spiral candlesticks
Turned wooden base, eighteenth century.
$300-375 each

Kyal lamp
Bail handle for hanging, burned coal oil, American, c. mid- to late nineteenth century.

Tin wall candle holder or sconce
New England, c. 1800. **$250-300**

"Hog-scraper" candlestick
Made from sheet iron, c. early nineteenth century. **$135-160**

Sixty-tube tin candle mold
Possibly used by a traveling candle maker or chandler, c. mid-nineteenth century. **$300-385**

Kerosene wall or coach lamp
C. late nineteenth century. **$225-275**

Copper-and-brass food mold
Possibly English, c. early nineteenth century.   **$135-150**

Iron cooking pans or spiders
Early nineteenth century.   **$135-175** *each*

Stoneware pitcher
Sponge decorated, molded rather than hand-thrown, c. late nineteenth century. **$75-100**

Enterprise coffee grinder
Original paint, c. late nineteenth century. **$350-450**

Handy fruit press
Factory-made, c. early twentieth century. **$140-175**

Iron dippers
Rat-tail handles, American, eighteenth century. **$100-125 each**

Collection of molded stoneware butter crocks
Stenciled decoration, all originally had lids, c. late nineteenth to early twentieth century. **$35-50 each**

65

Elgin coffee mill or grinder
Original painted finish, c. late nineteenth century.   **$450-550**

Chopping knife
Iron with maple handle, c. 1900.   **$28-35**

Copper candy kettle
Iron handles, c. late nineteenth to early twentieth century.   **$250-300**

Pewter chargers or dinner plates
English, 12"-16" in diameter, various markings, nineteenth century.   **$235-400** *each*

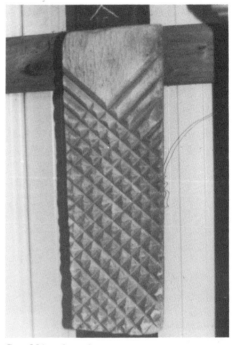

Scrubbing board
Pine, handcrafted, c. 1840-1860.   **$130-150**

Set of copper tavern measures
English, nineteenth century.
$1,200-1,500 for set of seven

Tin or tole tray
Decorated, American, c. late nineteenth century. **$175-250**

Factory-made tin pastry and food molds
C. 1880-1920. **$12-20**

Scrub or washboards
Factory-made, c. late nineteenth century to early twentieth century. **$45-75**

Tin strainer
Factory-made, c. 1880.   *$25-28*

Factory-made spice chest
Tin, painted gold with black lettering on the drawers, c. late nineteenth to early twentieth century.   *$145-155*

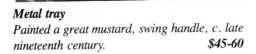

Metal tray
Painted a great mustard, swing handle, c. late nineteenth century.   *$45-60*

Lid from Badger Brand cranberry barrel
C. early twentieth century.   *$65-75*

Muffin mold
Cast iron, c. late nineteenth century.   **$35-45**

Muffin mold
Cast iron, c. 1850.   **$45-55**

Chocolate Molds

Chocolate molds have been used by candy manufacturers for more than a century to create candy in the shapes of American eagles, circus animals, fish, Santa Claus, Kewpie dolls, farm animals, Christmas trees, hearts, rabbits, shamrocks, cars, and people.

As local candy companies gradually went out of existence or consolidated in the early twentieth century, they sold many of their molds to antiques dealers and collectors.

The rarest of the company molds belong to the Hershey Corporation. The Hershey molds have seldom been made available to collectors and are always in demand.

The following chocolate molds are from the extensive collection of Betty and Jim Clark.

Bridesmaids	*$95*
Kewpie doll (large)	*$125*
Three little girls	*$75*

Liberty eagle on cannons	*$235*
Large fish	*$130*
Scotty dogs	*$70*

69

Unusual bear mold $185

Three witches (tray)	$60
Pumpkins	$85
Four witches	$75
Witch on a broom	$85

Squirrels	$65
Lambs	$95
Standing lamb	$75
Owl	$50
Seal	$50

Four bears in a row	$85
Four lions in a row	$85
Stalking lion	$55
Bear	$55
Elephant	$55

Turkey	$130
Large (10″) turkey	$210
Turkey	$85
Two turkeys	$60

Three ducks	$60
Large duck with hat and scarf	$135
Comic duck	$50
Duck on a nest	$50

Basket	$50
Eight hearts	$135
Tray of initials	$45

Two hens on a nest	$75
Large hen on a nest (10")	$70
Three hens on a nest	$70
Chick	$45

Rooster, 6½" high	$75
Hen	$50
Two roosters, 6½" high	$95
Mother hen	$65
Grim-looking rooster	$80

Hen, 15"	$275
Rooster	$65
Large rooster	$140

Santa with child and toys	$180
Small Santa (early)	$200
Santa on motorcycle	$125

Four old Santas (c. 1880)   *$165*
Small Santas   *$80*
Three old Santas   *$150*

Rabbit head   *$85*
Policeman   *$75*

*Santa with tree and toys in sleigh
pulled by deer*   *$175*

Santa (nineteenth century)   *$165*
Santa with sleigh and elf   *$175*
Four Santas   *$145*

Two 9" Santas   *$150*
Nineteenth-century Santa   *$175*
Santa with toy   *$85*
Rudolph   *$80*
Santa in sleigh   *$75*

Large (15") rabbit	$240
Rabbits pulling carts	$175
Standing rabbit	$55
Two rabbits pulling wagons	$45

Large (10") eggs	$140
Assorted eggs	$75

Rabbit on a basket	$80
Rabbits on sheet mold	$60
Rabbit riding a rooster	$50
Sitting rabbits	$50

Sheet mold of pineapples, birds, bells, socks
$80
Early (1880s), large egg $135

Rabbits riding roosters (6" high)	$75
Rabbit, 10" high	$95
Rabbit with egg in cart	$75

Boxing rabbit	$75
Rabbit with baby	$80
Mother rabbit	$65
Two rabbits with basket	$65

Graniteware

Note: This section was prepared by the officers of the American Graniteware Association.

Graniteware, also known as enamelware, agateware, porcelainware, glazedware, or speckleware, was a popular kitchenware from its first American production in the 1860s to 1930, when the marketing of aluminum caused its decline. Recently, the popularity of graniteware has been revived by collectors of country antiques.

As early as 1838, European countries were manufacturing graniteware. Mass production in the United States was initiated simultaneously by three companies in the 1860s. They were Vollrath of Sheboygan, Wisconsin; LaLance & Grosjean of Woodhaven, New York; and St. Louis Stamping Co. of St. Louis, Missouri. All three companies were quite successful and proud of their products' double- or triple-coated enameled surface over iron or steel base metals.

Old graniteware has escalated in value over the last two years, partly because of exposure in antiques publications and magazines that feature country furniture and decorative arts. Interior designers are using it more in home decorating, and increasing numbers of avid graniteware collectors are popping up across the country. Of course, a depletion of rare and mint pieces on the market also accounts for increased prices. In certain regions of the country such as the Southeast and Southwest, where graniteware is not as readily available, prices are generally higher.

In the present market, two types of graniteware collectors exist. One, the steadfast, long-time collector who invests time and money in search of unusual and mint pieces. And the other, a new collector in the graniteware market — the country and kitchenware collector who wishes to accessorize his home with graniteware. This trend has evolved because graniteware is available, affordable, and attractive. In addition, national exposure in country decorating magazines has given credibility to graniteware collecting.

The colors featured in country decorating magazines have influenced the new graniteware buyer. Popular colors are blue, cobalt blue, and gray. More unusual colors are green, brown, and copper red. Because of the great number of manufacturers, graniteware colors and decorations vary. Solid or shaded colors and the introduction of white through mottling, marbling, and speckling are examples of variations that may or may not influence a buyer's choice, depending on personal taste.

Graniteware includes a wide range of items, from pots and pans to toiletry items. Serious collectors search for rare examples such as pewter-trimmed pieces, butter churns, stoves, sinks, and dustpans. Some items are considered rare because of their color or limited quantities. For example, butter churns, declared unsafe for sanitary reasons by the federal government, were produced for only a short time.

With the depletion of rare examples, long-time graniteware collectors are beginning to acquire cross-collectibles such as advertising that features graniteware. Paper items available are magazine ads, premium cards, catalogues, cookbooks, instruction booklets, and cardboard signs. Trade cards are especially desirable. Advertising items made of graniteware include signs, cups, ashtrays, serving trays, and salesman's samples.

Other cross-collectibles include items made of graniteware and marked with identifying names or letters. Examples are railroad dishes bearing the initials of a particular company such as UPRR, and military items.

Because serious buyers want to learn more about their collection, pieces with either paper or stamped labels are considered more valuable. Oftentimes, a date is included on the label. Such pieces are prized by collectors.

Children's pieces and miniatures have always been avidly sought by graniteware and toy collectors. They command even higher prices in today's market. Miniatures were often used as toys, and children's pieces such as cups and plates were set in place on the table along with adult-size tableware.

Another graniteware collecting trend is to specialize in one type of item or in pieces of only one color. Coffeepots or teapots in various colors can make a most attractive display, and graniteware pieces of one color grouped together make a dramatic focal point in the home.

Since graniteware is still produced, it is important to distinguish between old and new. Check the gauge of the base metal. Generally, the heavier the steel or cast iron, the older the piece will be. Pieces with cast-iron handles can be dated 1870-1890. Those with wooden handles are c. 1900-1910. When searching for old graniteware, also look for seams, wooden knobs, and tin lids.

Pewter-trimmed, floral-design teapot
$125-175

Pewter-trimmed teapot   **$90-125**

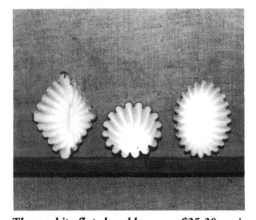

Three white fluted molds   **$25-30** *each*

Blue-gray speckled washboard   **$55-75**
Blue-gray speckled soap dish   **$25-30**

Gray wire muffin pan $30-55

Blue water pitcher $50-75

Blue sugar and creamer $40-75 *each*

Milk kettle with paper label $35-50

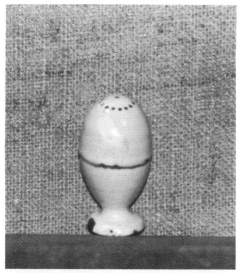

Salt shaker (rare)   *$35-45*

White fruit bowl   *$35-50*

Assorted miniatures   *$20-75 each*

Gray berlin pot with paper label   *$30-40*

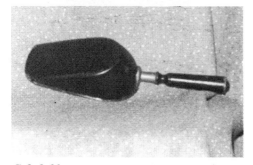

Cobalt blue scoop   *$50-75*

Gray batter bucket   *$55-70*

Gray domed serving tray   *$75-100*

Gray scale   *$55-80*

Gray dustpan (rare)   *$45-80*

Gray match holder   *$35-65*

Gray fluted mold, corn pattern   *$45-60*

Washing machine labeled NRA $20-35

Assorted soap dishes $25-60 *each*

Gray cocoa dipper $40-60

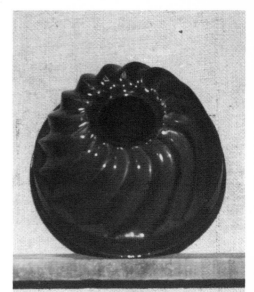

Cobalt blue Turk's-head mold $45-70

Brown-and-blue butter churn (rare)
$345-500

79

Cobalt blue water pail   *$40-75*

Child's ABC plate, cup, and saucer
$45-60 the set

Gray coffee urn with Savory label   *$75-150*

Advertising tray, "Calumet Baking Powder"
$35-55

White advertising pan, "Yeast Foam"
$15-25

Child's ABC table $70-90

Salesman's sample washpans with stamps
$35-45 each

Paper advertising Azure Blue Enamelware
$10-20

Close-up of stamped "Royal" label on
salesman's sample

Cardboard premium advertising sign $15-30

81

Cobalt syrup jug (rare) $50-75   *Cobalt blue miniature bowl and pitcher*
$50-75

3 Stoneware

Collectors of country stoneware must deal with a wide variety of merchandise and prices. To illustrate the diversity, we have stoneware items in this section that range from molded beer bottles available for less than $10, to spectacularly decorated pieces that sell for up to $10,000.

Dating Stoneware by Its Decoration

It is possible to estimate the age of a piece of stoneware by studying the techniques used to decorate it.

Incising

Stoneware was incised from the mid-eighteenth century until about 1830. In the 1740s, a stoneware pottery in Charlestown, Massachusetts, used simple, incised or "scratched" decorations on their pieces. Incising involved drawing or scratching designs into the soft clay with a pointed stick or piece of metal. It was a time-consuming process that became too expensive as competition increased in the early nineteenth century. A good example of incising is this miniature jug, a premium given away by the Cash Store of Altoona, Pennsylvania.

Painting

Painting birds, scenes, or casual swirls on stoneware replaced incising in the 1820s and 1830s and was commonly used until about 1890. The period between 1865 and 1880 was the golden age of decorating with a brush, with the most elaborate work produced by potteries in New York State and New England. Brush painting also became too costly when competition, new inventions, and changing customer tastes closed many of the smaller potteries and forced the survivors to produce stoneware as inexpensively as possible.

Stamping

Stamps, usually used to impress potters' marks on stoneware crocks, were made from metal, clay, or wood. On occasion, type from a printer's shop was utilized for a stamp.

This potter's mark was impressed into the side of the jar.

Slip-Trailing

In the 1840s and 1850s, the process of slip-cupping or trailing was used in some areas. A trail of slip (a creamy mixture of white clay combined with ground cobalt and water) was left on the surface of the stoneware. This became too costly for most stoneware makers and the process was discontinued.

The raised trail of slip drizzled from a quill stuck in a slip-cup can easily be felt on the surface of a piece so decorated.

This miniature jug is an example of slip-trailing.

Stenciling

The potteries began to use stencils in the late 1870s and continued until about 1920. A stencil was placed against the crock or jug and a brush dipped in cobalt-slip combination was run across it. Potteries in West Virginia and western Pennsylvania made extensive use of stenciled motifs on their wares.

The era of spectacular decoration ended when competition forced potteries to turn out large quantities of stoneware as cheaply as possible. When decorators were paid by the piece rather than by the day, there was little motivation to execute finely detailed scenes, animals, or human figures.

A buyer or business could still order a special piece decorated to his tastes, but this was not common and relatively few significant examples have survived.

Dating Stoneware by Its Manufacturer

Certain stoneware manufacturers were in business for a limited time. Their pieces can be dated through knowledge of the company's history.

The most collectible decorated stoneware crocks and jugs were produced in Bennington, Vermont, by various combinations of the Norton and Fenton families. The pottery was in operation in Bennington for almost a century. It is possible to date a piece with some accuracy by studying the owner's mark and checking when that particular owner was in possession of the pottery. For example, the longest single period of ownership was from 1861-1881, under the control of E. and L. P. Norton. Thus, any piece marked with those names was made during the twenty years of their ownership.

In contrast, the J. Norton and Co. mark was used only from 1859-1861, which limits the time span considerably. Other Bennington marks can be dated as follows:

Bennington Factory   pre-1823
L. Norton and Co.   1823-1828
L. Norton   1828-1833
L. Norton and Son   1833-1838
Julius Norton*   1838-1844
Norton and Fenton   1844-1847
Julius Norton*   1847-1850
J. and E. Norton   1850-1859
J. Norton & Co.   1859-1861
E. and L. P. Norton   1861-1881
E. Norton & Co.   1883-1894
The Edw'd Norton Co.   1886-1894

* The Julius Norton (1838-1844) jugs tend to

be more ovoid (pear-shaped) than the later (1847-1850) versions bearing the same mark.

It is possible to check other marks for their dates, as well. John Ramsay's *American Potters and Pottery* (Hale, Cushman, and Flint), published in 1939, and Webster's *Decorated Stoneware of North America* (1971) both contain extensive lists of potteries and their dates of operation.

It is important to keep the dating of stoneware in perspective. For example, potteries did not begin to stencil their products on January 1, 1878, nor did they all stop in 1920. Some isolated country potteries continued brush painting until almost 1900, while others stopped in the 1870s and chose a quicker and less costly method. In general, though, the following time frame will help you date stoneware pieces.

1740   First American stoneware pottery begins operation at Charlestown, Massachusetts.
1800   Incising is the primary technique for decorating stoneware.
1815   Norton Pottery at Bennington produces stoneware.
1825   Erie Canal opens up new stoneware markets and increases competition.
1840   Bennington introduces Rockingham glazes.
1840s   Glass products become affordable and the stoneware market suffers.
1860s-1880   The finest examples of brush-decorated stoneware are produced.
1880s-1920   Much of the decorated stoneware is stenciled.
1890s   Crown top or cap improves sealing on glass bottles, killing the market for stoneware soda and beer bottles.
1919   Prohibition of alcohol destroys demand for whiskey jugs.

For more information on stoneware, send for the annual catalogue of The 3 Behrs, RFD 8, Horsepound Road, Carmel, New York 10512. The Behrs have been sending out illustrated catalogues of their stoneware for the past thirteen years and have sold stoneware by mail order to collectors in each of the fifty states. Behrs' catalogue is sent to prospective buyers in January. They also publish two supplements during the course of each calendar year. Inquiries about the catalogue should be made from October to December.

Another fine source of information on stoneware is Willard Grande of Saratoga Springs, New York, one of the nation's premier collectors of nineteenth-century decorated stoneware. A portion of his extensive collection is on display at the recently opened Museum of Antiques and Art of Saratoga Springs. This is located at 153 Regent Street and is open daily. Grande also has a shop where more than two hundred pieces of stoneware from his collection are for sale.

Four-gallon crock
Ottman Bros., Fort Edward, New York, dated 1874, with name of the pottery and its location impressed into the top of the crock. The "4" (capacity mark) was also impressed. If it had been drawn with a sharp stick or pointed metal rod, it would have been incised. The cobalt wreath and the "1874" were brush painted. A painted wreath with a date was also used by J. Norton and Company of Bennington, Vermont, between 1859-1861.

Unmarked Pennsylvania storage jar
Brush-painted decoration, c. 1880. Brush decoration was made with cobalt slip. The "4" is a capacity mark and the trailing vine circles the jar.

Two-gallon crock
Somerset Pottery, with stenciled "handshake," c. late nineteenth century.

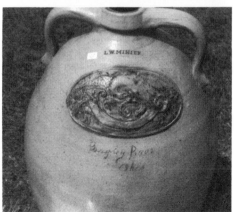

Five-gallon crock

J. & E. Norton, Bennington, Vermont, c. 1850-1859, has flower spray made with a slip-cup. This was produced at Bennington during a period that many collectors feel was the pottery's finest for the quality of decoration. The Bennington decorators created several types of flower sprays in varying degrees of complexity.

Double-handle cooler

"L. W. Minier" impressed into the neck, c. 1850. A plaster-of-paris mold was used to create the American eagle scene from clay. The scene then was stuck on with a small amount of thick slip. This technique of applied decoration is called "sprigging" and is not commonly found on country stoneware.

Stoneware pitcher

Unmarked, decorated with a sponge dipped in slip, c. 1870.

Two-gallon jug
Unmarked, but probably from Pennsylvania. **$200-235**

One-gallon jug
J. & E. Norton, Bennington, Vermont.
$700-800

Two-gallon jug
White's, Utica, New York. **$300-400**

One-gallon jug
Thompson & Tyler, Troy, New York. **$550-650**

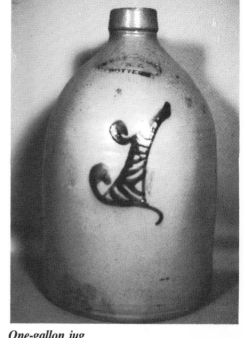

One-gallon jug
Marked "Keene, N.H."   ***$375-425***

One-gallon jug
West Troy Pottery, New York.   ***$165-195***

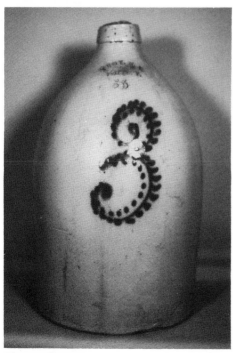

Three-gallon jug
West Troy Pottery, New York.   ***$165-195***

Two-gallon jug
J. & E. Norton, Bennington, Vermont.
          $325-425

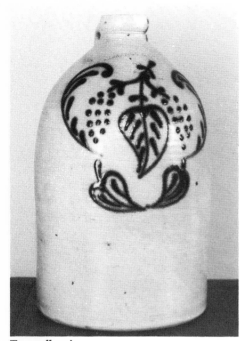

Two-gallon jug
Edmonds & Company, Boston, Massachusetts.
$350-375

Four-gallon jug
New York Stoneware Company, Fort Edward,
New York.   *$750-850*

Two-gallon jug
Wm. E. Warner, West Troy, New York.
$200-225

Three-gallon crock
Unmarked.   *$275-335*

Three-gallon crock
West Troy, New York.   *$335-395*

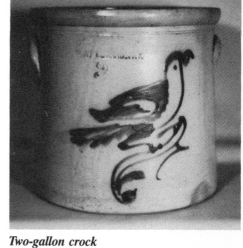

Two-gallon crock
Ottman Bros., Fort Edward, New York.
                              $295-355

One-gallon crock
Unmarked.   *$395-425*

Two-gallon crock
Ballard Brothers, Burlington, Vermont.
                              $175-225

One-gallon crock
Unmarked, but probably from Somerset,
Massachusetts.   *$395-425*

Five-gallon crock
Unmarked, but probably from New York State.   **$200-250**

Three-gallon crock
Haxstun & Company, Fort Edward, New York.
                                                $575-750

Two-gallon crock
J. Norton & Co., Bennington, Vermont.
                                                $550-650

One-gallon crock
Unmarked.   **$135-155**

One and one half gallon crock
J. & E. Norton, Bennington, Vermont.
                                                $325-375

Three-gallon crock
Unmarked, but probably from Poughkeepsie, New York, rare "dog" decoration.
$850-1,000

Three-gallon crock
Unmarked. **$325-375**

Two-gallon crock
Poughkeepsie, New York. **$225-275**

Six-quart crock
Unmarked. **$235-300**

One-gallon crock
White's, Utica, New York. **$150-175**

93

One-quart canning jars
Pennsylvania.   *$135-150 each*

One-gallon storage jar
Pennsylvania.   *$150-175*

One- and two-gallon preserve or canning jars
Pennsylvania.   *$150-275 each*

One-half-pint pitcher
Unmarked, Pennsylvania "tanware."
                              $475-575

Two-gallon pitcher
Pennsylvania, unmarked.   *$700-900*

One-gallon batter pail
Unsigned.   *$335-395*

Two-gallon pitcher
Unmarked.   *$375-425*

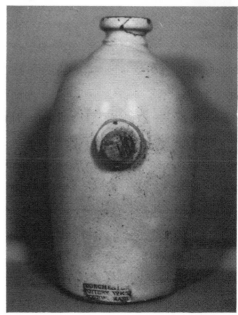

Foot warmer
Covered with white Bristol glaze, Dorchester Pottery Works, Boston, Massachusetts.
          $55-75

95

Foot warmer
Covered with brown Albany slip, West Troy
Pottery. **$55-75**

Four-gallon butter churn
Unmarked, but probably from Dorchester
Pottery Works; horse design on both sides.
$800-1,200

Five-gallon butter churn
J. & E. Norton, Bennington, Vermont.
$775-975

Four-gallon butter churn
F. Woodworth, Burlington, Vermont.
                                    $265-335

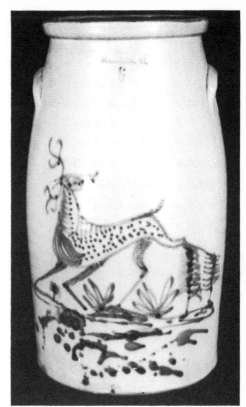

Six-gallon butter churn
O. L. & A. K. Ballard, Burlington, Vermont.   ***$2,900-3,500***

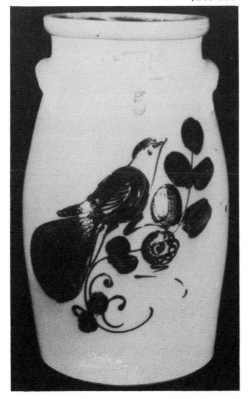

Five-gallon butter churn
White's, Utica, New York.   ***$750-900***

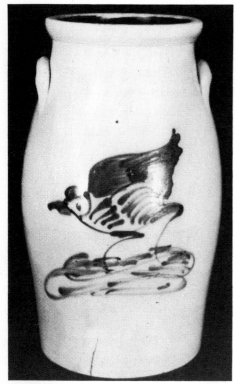

Four-gallon butter churn
Unmarked, pecking chicken.   **$700-800**

Sleepy Eye molded stoneware vase
$225-300

Sleepy Eye Flour premium
Molded stoneware salt bowl.   **$375-425**

Sleepy Eye molded stoneware butter crock
$450-550

Sleepy Eye bronze paperweight
Given as a premium.   **$700-900**

Six-gallon butter churn
Fulper Brothers Pottery, Flemington, New Jersey, c. 1880. This is a finely detailed scene of two birds resting on branches. The ear handles were applied to the churn after it was turned on the potter's wheel. The Fulper family was in the pottery business in the Flemington area for almost the entire nineteenth century.   **$2,000-2,500**

Cardboard fan
Sleepy Eye Milling Company.   **$200-225**

Six-gallon butter churn
John Burger, Rochester, New York, c. 1860. Has zebra-striped deer similar in form to the classic Bennington deers from the Norton potteries in Vermont. The Fort Edward Pottery Company from Fort Edward, New York, also produced a similar deer with groundcover and spruce trees in the 1860s. **$4,000-5,500**

Six-gallon butter churn
T. Harrington, Lyons, New York, has slip-cup scene and capacity mark, c. 1860.
$3,000-3,500

Six-gallon butter churn
J. Burger, Rochester, New York, features an Indian brave surrounded by a floral wreath, c. 1880. Human figures or faces that have been brushed or slip-cupped on stoneware are rare. **$3,500-4,000**

Three-gallon ovoid jug
Marked Commeraws/Stoneware/Corlears/Hook/N. York, c. 1800. The impressed row of swags and pendants circles the jug. This type of decoration took a great deal of time because each swag and pendant was added individually with a hand stamp. Thomas Commeraws was a potter in New York City in the late eighteenth and early nineteenth century.

$3,500-4,500

Ovoid jug
Lyman and Clark, Gardiner, Maine, c. 1838. Alanson Lyman and Decius Clark operated a pottery in Gardiner in the late 1830s and early 1840s. The brushed decoration on this piece was done with brown ocher slip. It is uncommon because of the date decoration.

$800-1,000

Four-gallon crock
A. D. Whittemore, Havana, New York, c. 1875. **$3,500-4,000**

Three-gallon crock
Fort Edward Pottery Co., c. 1860. Features scene that could best be described as of a "scarecrow in the garden." **$2,500-3,500**

Twelve-gallon jar
N. A. White and Son, Utica, New York, c. 1884. Noah White's decorators used several variations of this orchid, executed in thick cobalt with a slip cup. This is not necessarily a rare motif on stoneware, but is less common on a twelve-gallon jar than on the more conventional two- to four-gallon sizes.
$2,000-2,500

Six-gallon crock
Haxstun and Ottman, Fort Edward, New York. **$3,500-4,500**

Three gallon crock
J. & E. Norton, c. 1855. This spectacularly decorative crock has a slip-cupped rooster, spruce tree, fence, and three houses. Pieces that are this elaborately decorated were generally specially ordered at the factory.
$3,500-4,500

Six-gallon crock
C. W. Braun, Buffalo, New York, c. 1865. The decorators who painted birds, swirls, and flowers on stoneware allowed their imaginations free rein. It is often difficult to determine if a bird is a robin, dove, or bluebird, because the artists borrowed a beak from one species and a body from another to create their unique birds. This slip-cupped bird may be a grouse. **$2,200-3,000**

Six-gallon crock

A. O. Whittemore, Havana, New York, c. 1875. This illustrates a point about stoneware decorators' imaginations. The artist who slip-cupped this tropical scene had probably never been south of Binghamton. **$2,200-2,800**

Six-gallon crock

Seymour Bosworth, Hartford, Connecticut, c. 1880. Henry Seymour and Stanley Bosworth were in the stoneware business in the Hartford area from the early 1870s to the mid-1890s. **$3,200-3,800**

"Starburst" crocks

T. Harrington, Lyons, New York, c. 1865. Thomas Harrington's starburst or eight-pointed star was used at his pottery in Lyons, New York, in the early 1860s. A number of variations of this basic design were made by potteries at Jordan, New York, Cortland, New York, and Bennington, Vermont. The four-gallon, "man in the moon" starburst may be unique. The Cowden and Wilcox Pottery of Harrisburg, Pennsylvania, did a design with a man surrounded with a wreath rather than a moon.

"Sun smiles," five-gallon: **$1,500-2,000**
"Man in the moon," four-gallon:

$2,000-3,000
"Half moon," three-gallon: **$1,500-2,000**

Six-gallon crock
Fort Edward Pottery Co., c. 1860. Features an elaborate representation of a peacock. Take special note of the detail in the fence and groundcover. **$1,800-2,200**

Three-gallon crock
White's, Utica, New York, c. 1870. The castle on an island with a rocky cliff in the foreground makes this an incredibly rare piece of decorated stoneware. **$3,500-4,500**

Two-gallon crock and pitcher
F. T. Wright and Son, Taunton, Massachusetts, c. 1870. The two birds were done by the same decorator. It is not uncommon to see similar birds from different potteries because the itinerant decorators often moved from pottery to pottery. The decorated pitcher is rare.
Pitcher: **$1,000-1,400**
Crock: **$500-700**

Three-gallon crock
W. A. Macquoid and Co./Pottery Works/Little W. 12th St., New York, c. 1865. The phrase under the sailing ship reads, "Don't Give up the Ship! Capt. Law." Historically, that statement is credited to Captain Lawrence. This could have been a presentation piece for a Civil War naval officer upon his return home. **$4,500-5,500**

Five-gallon crock
Harrington and Burger, Rochester, New York,
c. 1853. **$4,000-5,000**

Four-gallon crock
W. A. Lewis, Gatesville, New York, c. 1855.
This is a slip-cupped illustration of the Gates-
ville Pottery, in which the crock was made. It
is the only known piece of decorated stone-
ware that depicts a pottery. **$7,000-10,000**

Six-gallon crock
W. A. Macquoid, New York City, c. 1865. This
American eagle and shield were probably
done in a moment of patriotic fervor toward
the end of the Civil War. **$4,000-5,000**

Molded Stoneware

Note: This section was written by George Schnitzer, Jr., of Nashville, Tennessee.

It wasn't until the late nineteenth century that mass-produced, molded stoneware was available in this country. Molded stoneware differed from earlier hand-formed pieces in that standard, uniform sizes could be manufactured repeatedly. Labels, too, could be reproduced for easy identification, advertising, and marketing.

Merchants sold beverages of every kind in molded returnable bottles and jugs. Housewives bought molded canning jars and butter churns. And grocers sold a variety of products in modern molded stoneware as America moved into the twentieth century. The soft drink industry was developing, and ginger beer and mineral water in molded containers followed English and Scottish immigrants to the northeast.

Throughout the mid-1800s, most molded stoneware came from Britain, where manufacturing was a major industry. A fine example of this is the Moerlein Gerst Lager Beir sold in Nashville, Tennessee, in bottles made in Glasgow, Scotland, in 1889-1890. More than a dozen British manufacturers were still in operation in the early part of the twentieth century.

Molded stoneware was popular because it kept beverages cool and was almost unbreakable. This outweighed the fact that it was heavy, hard to clean, and expensive to produce. It was not until the development of the icebox and the economical mass-production of glass that the popularity of molded stoneware declined.

Dating Molded Stoneware

The shapes and sizes of bottles, jugs, and jars usually reflected the amount of product contained and the type of stopper used. It is the stopper that helps to date the stoneware. Traditionally, molded stoneware was gray, brown, or honey, depending on the glaze and clay used. In the late 1800s, Albany slip and Bristol glaze were used. In the early 1900s, competition among merchants was fierce, and they would do anything affordable to distinguish their product. This meant producing dark green, burnt orange, brick red, mid-brown, cobalt blue, and even pink stoneware. These colors are considered rare and exceptional additions to a collection.

Collecting Molded Stoneware

Collecting molded stoneware offers the opportunity for specialization. Collectors often single out bottles, jugs, or jars; certain beverages or food products; geographical locations; or industrial products. There seems to be something for everyone — even those with a limited budget.

Molded stoneware traditionally has not been as collectible as the early country pieces, which command high prices from collectors. But in the past few years, this has changed. At bottle shows, flea markets, and fine antiques shows throughout the country, collectors have begun to recognize molded stoneware as interesting, collectible Americana. Ten years ago, an average jug could be purchased for $15, or a bottle for $5. Today, that same jug sells for $50 and the bottle for $20. American bottles generally are worth about 25 percent more than foreign ones.

The following photos illustrate some of the types of products and pieces of molded stoneware actively sought by collectors today. It should be noted that the bottles, jars, and jugs shown were selected to illustrate a variety of shapes, labeling techniques, and stoppers. Many collectible bottles can be purchased from $8-100. These are typical examples of the more common pieces that can be found at local flea markets, bottle shows, and antiques shops.

Old Jug Lager

The Moerlein Gerst Brewing Company, Nashville, Tennessee, c. 1889-1890. Tan tops, white bases, transfers, corks.

Tennessee state seal (pint):	**$40**
Rooster trademark (pint):	**$50**
Rooster trademark (quart):	**$75**

Four types of stoppers

One-pint English Brewed Ginger Beer, McCoy & Hanlon, Watertown, New York, c. 1900. Tan top, white base, transfer, cork, blob top. **$20**

Home Brewed Ginger Beer, Rye Mineral Water Works, Rye, England, c. 1915. Tan top, white base, transfer, internal screw thread, blob top. **$15**

Ten-ounce English Brewed Ginger Beer, Con. Murphy, Syracuse, New York, c. 1925. Tan top, white base, transfer, crown cap. **$20**

One-pint Stone Ginger Beer, Robertson's, Montrose, Scotland, c. 1910. Dark tan top, white base, transfer, lightning swing. **$20**

Moerlein's Old Jug Lager

The Christian Moerlein Brewing Company, Cincinnati, Ohio, c. 1888-1889. Tan tops, white bases, transfers, corks.

Quart:	**$75**
Pint:	**$40**

One-pint Paterson's Best Stone Ginger
W. R. Paterson L.T.D., Glasgow, Scotland, c.
1925. Tan top, white base, transfer, crown
cap, unusual shape. **$18**

One-pint Old English Stone Ginger Beer
Clayton's, London, England, c. 1925.
Mid-brown, white base, transfer, crown cap,
unusual color. **$24**

One-pint Old English Ginger Beer
Sussex Beverage Company, Sussex, N. B.,
Canada, c. 1925. White, transfer, crown
cap. **$20**

Ten-ounce Stone Fizz
The Stone Fizz Company of America, Chat-
tanooga, Tennessee, c. 1922. Tan top, white
base, transfer, crown cap. **$20**

One-pint Yong Fung Company
Hong Kong and Tien Tsing, China, c. 1930.
Tan top, white base, transfer, cork. **$20**

One-pint T. Laughton
Scarborough, England, Galtee More, honey
color, transfer, c. 1910. **$20**

One-pint Old Style Ginger Beer
E. Smithwick and Sons, Kilkenny, Ireland,
Galtee More, honey color, transfer, c.
1910. **$20**

One-pint Target Brand Ginger Beer
The Scarborough & Whitby Breweries, LD.,
Scarborough, England, Galtee More, honey
color, transfer, c. 1910. **$20**

One-quart Castle Bottling Stores
W. Atkinson & Sons, Helmsley, England, c.
1910. Tan top, white base, transfer, lightning
swing. **$40**

One-quart Grumman's Bottling Works
So. Norwalk, Connecticut, c. 1900. White,
transfer, lightning swing. **$40**

Eleven-and-a-half-ounce Stone Ginger Beer
Josiah Russell's, New York, New York, c. 1930. Brown, paper label (shoulder impressed), crown cap.   **$15**

One-pint Stone Brewed Ginger Beer
Townsend's, Salford, England, c. 1900. Honey, impressed, cork, blob top.   **$15**

Ginger Beer
W. Biscombe, Plymouth, England, c. 1915. White, transfer, internal screw thread, print, blob top.   **$15**

One-quart 1879 Old Jug Whiskey
Freiberg Bros., Cincinnati, Ohio, c. 1900. Tan top, white base, transfer, cork.   **$45**

One-pint Lawson's, Hardman, Limited
Manchester, England, c. 1925. Tan top, white base, transfer, crown cap, "dumpy" shape.
$15

One-pint J. Ellis & Co.
Wakefield, England, c. 1900. Tan top, white base, impressed, cork, "dumpy" shape.   **$15**

One-pint Brewed Ginger Beer
Smith and Clody, Buffalo, New York, c. 1910.
White, transfer, cork. **$15**

John's English Brew
Southern English Ginger Beer Co., Jacksonville, Florida, c. 1900. White, transfer, cork,
"stumpy" (short pint). **$30**

One-pint IDRIS
Brown, impressed, crown cap, long neck,
unusual shape, c. 1925. **$10**

One-pint Brewed Ginger Beer
Vartray, Buffalo, New York, c. 1925. Dark
brown, white base, transfer, probably lightning swing, unusual shape. **$20**

One-pint Salt & Co.
Burton-on-Trent, c. 1920. White, transfer,
cork, unusual shape. **$15**

One-pint Brewed Ginger Beer
Vartray, Buffalo, New York, c. 1900. Tan top,
white base, transfer, cork. **$20**

One-pint Ginger Beer
T. F. Adams & Sons, Halstead, England, c.
1910. Tan top, white base, transfer, internal
screw thread. **$22**

**Oversized-pint Fermented Stone Ginger
Beer/Non-Intoxicant**
Brewster & Dodgson, Leeds, England, c.
1910. Tan top, white base, transfer, internal
screw thread. **$22**

One-pint Hurst Cross/Herb Beers
Lees's, Hurst, England, c. 1910. Tan top,
white base, transfer, internal screw thread.
$22

Ten-ounce High Grade European Style Ginger Beer
New York Bottling Works, Syracuse, New York, c. 1920. Dark brown top, white base, transfer, crown cap. **$20**

Seven-and-a-half-ounce Old Style Stone Bottle Ginger Beer
Diehl's, Nashville, Tennessee, c. 1920. Dark brown top, white base, transfer, crown cap. **$20**

One-pint Mineral Water Manufacturers
E. Smithwick & Sons, Ltd., Kilkenny, Ireland, c. 1920. Honey, transfer, crown cap. **$15**

Eight-ounce Old Fashioned Root Beer
C. Leary & Co., Newbury Port, Massachusetts, c. 1920. Dark brown top, white base, transfer, crown cap. **$20**

Nine-ounce Jacob Guttenberg
Medina, New York, c. 1920. White, transfer, crown cap. **$15**

Ten-ounce English Brewed Ginger Beer
Con. Murphy, Syracuse, New York, c. 1920. Tan top, white base, transfer, crown cap. **$20**

Two-gallon Old Peerless jug
M. Ryan, Nashville, Tennessee, c. 1900. Dark brown top, white base, transfer. **$40**

One-gallon Groceries and Liquors Jug
B. W. Hooper & Bro., Nashville, Tennessee, c. 1900. Dark brown top, white base, transfer. **$50**

One-pint Vallance
Sidmouth, England, c. 1915. Dark green top, white base (very rare color), transfer, lightning swing.   **$70**

One-pint Vallance
Sidmouth, England, c. 1910. Dark green top, white base (very rare color), transfer, internal screw thread.   **$65**

One-pint J. Mills & Sons
London, England, c. 1900. Tan top, white base, transfer, cork, "beehive" blob top (made only by this manufacturer).   **$20**

One-pint J. Mills & Sons
London, England, c. 1910. Brown, impressed, internal screw thread, champagne shape, "beehive" blob top.   **$20**

One-pint J. Mills & Sons
London, England, c. 1900. Brown, impressed, cork, "beehive" blob top.   **$15**

One-half-gallon Chas. Zickler & Co. jug
Nashville, Tennessee, c. 1900. Dark brown top, white base, transfer, rounded shoulder.
$55

One-half-gallon Wholesale Whiskies & Wines jug
Montgomery & Clark, Nashville, Tennessee, c. 1900. Dark brown top, white base, transfer, rounded shoulder.   **$40**

Shaker #7 rocking chair
Cushion rail, Mt. Lebanon, New York, c. 1880.   *$1,200-1,400*

Leather fire bucket
New England, c. 1835.   *$450-500*

Bennington stoneware pottery
Rockingham glaze, mid-nineteenth century.   *$450-650*

Hanging chest   *$250-375*

Advertising tins
Manufactured early twentieth century.   *$55-85 each*

Tumbling clown toy
Hand-carved pine, painted, c. 1870. $65-75

New England country basket
Oak splint, painted blue, c. 1850.   *$300-375*

Chip-carved butter print
From Pennsylvania, c. 1840.   *$150-175*

Maple "work" bowl, c. 1860.   *$275-300*

Tin candle molds and pewter candlestick
All nineteenth century.   **$125-500**

Child's sled
Made in Maine. Original stenciled decoration, c. 1900. **$200-250**

Hand-stitched crib quilt
Early twentieth century. **$140-200**

Pine candle lantern
Twig handle, c. 1870.   **$200-275**

One-gallon Thompson Springs Mineral Water jug
A. W. Thompson Sons, Nashville, Tennessee, c. 1920. White, blue and white lines, transfer. **$50**

One-gallon Calmalith Mineral Water jug
Calmdale Farm, Nashville, Tennessee, c. 1900. White, transfer, rounded shoulder. **$50**

One-half-gallon Divine, Clear, Mount, Water jug
Ed H. Liner, Propr., Nashville, Tennessee, c. 1910. White, transfer. **$40**

One-quart Wholesale Dealers in Groceries & Liquors jug
Connor & Brady, Nashville, Tennessee, c. 1920. Tan top, white base, transfer, rounded shoulder. **$30**

Seven-inch-tall canning jar
Wax sealer, dark brown, no markings, c. 1890. **$10**

Eight-inch-tall canning jar
Wax sealer, reddish brown, no markings, c. 1890. **$10**

Seven-inch-tall canning jar
McComb Pottery & Co., screw-on cap, white, c. 1900. **$15**

Stoneware canning jars
The Weir #5 and The Weir #4; patented March 1, 1892, and April 18, 1901. White, cam-lever closure, c. 1905. **$25-45**

Stoneware canning jars
The Weir (one pint to one-half gallon); patented March 1, 1892. Dark brown top, white base, cam-lever closure, c. 1895. The Weir jar was made in a variety of sizes in white and two-tone. **$25-45**

Five-gallon Red Wing jar
Red Wing Stoneware Co., Red Wing, Minnesota, c. 1900. White, red wing transfer, cam-lever closure, wire bail handle. **$50**

4 Baskets

A collector can spend the better part of a lifetime studying the regional differences and construction techniques of American country baskets and still not be an authority. But, by reading a few books on baskets, observing and discussing baskets at antiques shows, and taking a periodic trip to a museum that houses a complete basket collection (e.g., Landus Valley Farm Museum near Lancaster, Pennsylvania), you can become fairly knowledgeable in a relatively brief period of time.

If you are going to collect baskets, it is not critical to have an abundant background on the subject. Dealers will be happy to help you if you show an interest. But it does help to understand some basic basketry terms.

Swing handle — This is exactly what it implies. The handle can move freely within the constraints of the "bow" at each end of the basket. Swing-handle baskets are normally more difficult to find and more expensive to purchase than the more conventional fixed-handle baskets. Like bail handles, swing handles are usually found on baskets that were used to transport small packages or groceries from the store to the home. The handles allowed bulky items to be placed in and taken out of the basket.

Fixed handle — A handle that is permanently bound to the sides of the basket may be described as "fixed." The majority of baskets have fixed handles.

"Potato" stamp decoration — Few country baskets were decorated because they were usually designed for utilitarian purposes and not for display. However, the Algonkian and the Iroquois Indians did decorate their simple splint baskets.

They carved a design into a potato or a piece of soft wood, dipped it in dye made from vegetables or plants, and firmly pressed the design against the basket's splint. The simple decoration was typically a geometric design. The Indians sold these baskets to tourists in New England, Minnesota, and Wisconsin until well into the twentieth century.

The storage basket pictured has potato stamp decoration on its sides and on the cover.

"Kicked in" bottom — The purpose of a "kicked in," demijohn, or raised bottom was to evenly distribute the contents of the basket to its sides. These baskets were made specifically to carry heavy loads.

Melon basket — This Indian-made basket takes its name from its similarity to a halved watermelon. It was designed to be a multipurpose basket, used for carrying garden vegetables or bringing the mail home from the post office.

Note how the splint weavers are woven up and under each of the "ribs" in this basket.

Wicker — Most wicker or willow baskets were machine made in the late nineteenth or early twentieth century. The willow sticks or rods that were used in furniture and basket making were pliable, durable, and easily found. This wicker basket is presently worth about $12-20. It was mass-produced sometime between 1920-1940.

Cheese basket — A cheese basket was used to separate curds from whey. To do this, the basket, lined with a cheesecloth filter, was placed on top of a large stoneware crock. When the mixture of curds and whey was poured through the basket, the curds stayed in the cloth and the whey ran into the crock.

This style of basket may be the most sought after by collectors. Cheese baskets range from 8″ to 36″ in diameter. Their hexagonal pattern was also used in the construction of herb drying baskets.

As you begin your basket collection, you'll find that most American splint (split) baskets were made from oak or ash. However, you may run across some examples of Nantucket "light ship" baskets. These were woven from rattan imported from the Philippines and were first made on the South Shoal Light Ship about 1855-1860. Other than the Nantucket baskets, it is unusually difficult to isolate the geographic area in which a particular basket was made.

Dating Baskets

Basket construction techniques changed little from the early nineteenth to early twentieth centuries. This creates problems for collectors attempting to date their baskets. Also, country baskets were often exposed to bad weather and heavy use, prematurely adding years to their appearance.

Determining a Basket's Value

Baskets in common styles have *not* increased significantly in demand or value in recent years. Their condition is still the critical factor in determining value.

Uncommon basket styles (cheese, herb drying, swing-handled) have escalated in value, although not as quickly as they did between 1975-1980.

Trends in Basket Making

The market for handcrafted baskets was destroyed in the late nineteenth century by the invention of a veneering machine that produced bands of splint. Individual basket makers could not compete with the factories, which produced and sold less expensive baskets.

In recent years, though, there has been a dramatic increase in the number of crafts people who skillfully hand-produce country baskets. They do not weave their baskets to deceive potential buyers. Instead, they provide an option for people who want country baskets, but can't bring themselves to pay $200 for an antique when they can buy a newly made version for $65. The craftsmanship of these new baskets is often exceptional, and the price is certainly right. Eventually, many of these baskets will acquire patina and will be equally as coveted as the nineteenth-century baskets.

Cheese basket
Oak splint, 26" in diameter, New England, nineteenth century. **$475-600**

Swing-handle basket
Oak splint, double-wrapped rim, New England, c. late nineteenth century. The intricate wrapping on the handle of this basket is unusual. **$275-335**

Wall basket
Ash splint, single-wrapped rim, carved hickory bow, twentieth century. **$75-100**

Covered storage hamper
Oak splint, nineteenth century. **$85-125**

Potato-stamped storage basket
Indian-made, New England, probably had a lid, c. early twentieth century. **$65-75**

Oak splint grocery basket
Double swing or bail handles, double-wrapped rim, c. late nineteenth century. **$65-85**

Potato-stamped basket
Indian-made, New England, c. early twentieth century. The bow handles on this basket are not capable of supporting much weight. The basket was probably designed to display fruits or vegetables on a table. **$75-100**

Unusual ovoid oak splint basket
Rib construction, carved and notched handle, New England, nineteenth century. **$160-200**

Ox muzzle
Thick oak splint and hickory ribs, New England, c. mid-nineteenth century. **$60-90**

Apple-drying basket
New England, 2½' × 4', rare style, c. mid-nineteenth century. Sliced apples were placed in the basket and allowed to dry in the sun.
$300-450

Log or kindling carrying basket
Hickory handle, oak splint, twentieth century.
$75-85

Splint laundry/wash basket
Oak splint, early twentieth century.
$55-65

Fixed-handle utility basket
Nine inches in diameter, unusual rim nailed to the individual ribs of the basket, New England, nineteenth century.
$110-125

Miniature melon basket

Rib construction, ash splint, 4" in diameter, New England, nineteenth century. This basket is especially well made and has acquired a great patina over the years. Miniature baskets are hard to find and command high prices.

$135-150

Swing-handle basket

Reinforced bottom, New England, probably used for carrying vegetables or produce, 14" in diameter, nineteenth century. **$235-260**

Picnic basket or hamper

Plaited or checker-work construction, white oak splint, twentieth century. **$50-65**

Utility basket

Oak splint, "over and under" construction, single-wrapped rim, carved handle, 6" in diameter, nineteenth century. "Over and under" or plaiting is one of the simplest techniques used in making baskets. **$60-75**

Tightly woven utility basket

Rib construction, oak splint, nineteenth century. Note how the splint handle is "x bound" to the rim of the basket for extra stability.

$85-100

Bushel-type basket
Factory-made, bail handle, reinforced rim, twentieth century. **$45-60**

Field basket
Ash splint "buttocks" bottom, 33" long, nineteenth century. **$300-375**

Field basket
White oak splint, "notched" bow handles, New England, nineteenth century. **$125-150**

Field basket
White oak splint, used for gathering vegetables, reinforced sides and bottom, nineteenth century. **$135-150**

Field basket
Thick white oak splint, nailed to base and rim, painted, New England, nineteenth century.
$55-65

Storage basket
Unusual style, rib construction, 25" long, twisted hickory handle, c. late nineteenth century.　　　　　　　　　**$500-550**

"Buttocks" baskets
Oak splint, well made, c. early twentieth century.　　　　　　　**$75-100** *each*

Fixed-handle utility baskets
Tightly woven, oak splint.　　　　**$95-135**

"Buttocks" baskets
Variety of sizes, oak and ash splint.
$65-100 each

"Buttocks" basket
White oak splint, tightly woven, thick splint fixed handle, twentieth century. **$75-90**

Covered basket
Nine inches in diameter, ash splint, well-made, possibly Indian-made, nineteenth century.
$65-85

Covered basket
Checker-work weave on lid, plaited construction, possibly Indian-made, used for storage. **$75-100**

Clam basket
Ash splint, fixed-handle, open-weave bottom. **$55-75**

Utility basket
Woven square binds handle to the rest of the basket, Indian-made, twentieth century. **$45-60**

Laundry/wash basket
Double rim, carved bow handles, checker-work open bottom, oak splint. **$115-130**

Shaker basket
Carved heart-shaped handles, New England, nineteenth century. This type of basket would have been used for the short-term storage of fruits or vegetables. **$275-325**

Stack of berry baskets
Ash splint, c. mid-twentieth century. These baskets typify the standard factory-made, stapled products of the mid-twentieth century. **15-20¢ each**
59-69¢ each with berries

Interior of the Shaker basket
Checker-work bottom.

Field basket (on its side)
Oak splint, 32" in diameter, thickly carved bow handles. **$110-150**

Egg basket (hanging on left)
Fixed handle, ash splint, 7" in diameter, some breaks in the wrapping on the rim. **$45-55**

Swing-handle basket
New England, c. mid-nineteenth century.
$250-285

Bushel-type basket (far left)
White oak splint, carved bow handles, rib construction, tightly woven.   **$120-150**

Laundry/wash basket (second from right)
Carved bow handles, open-weave bottom, 18" × 30".   **$90-125**

Utility basket (far left)
Reinforced sides and bottom, fixed-handle, oak splint.   **$80-110**

Half-bushel basket (second from left)
Tightly woven, carved bow handles, rib construction.   **$120-145**

Swing-handle basket (center front)
Reinforced rim, wooden bottom, ash splint, late nineteenth to early twentieth century.
$115-140

Cheese basket (right)
Oak splint, 21" in diameter, New England.
$385-500

Covered basket
Oak splint, ash splint, used for storage, 11" in diameter.   **$75-100**

5 Shaker

In May of 1983, we had an opportunity to attend the American Heritage Antiques Show near Lancaster, Kentucky. The major question on the minds of many of the collectors and dealers at the show was how to distinguish Shaker furniture from simple country pieces marked "Shaker" or "Shaker-type." There are no secret techniques that knowledgeable collectors or dealers use to solve this dilemma. A key to making the correct decision is to buy intellectually, not emotionally.

Merely because a table, basket, or chair is labeled "Shaker" does not necessarily mean the attribution is correct. The dealer may be offering the item in good faith because he was told by the previous owner that it was originally from Mount Lebanon, New York, and had been given to the daughter of a nearby blacksmith who repaired the Shakers' farm implements.

It is almost impossible for experts to determine the precise Shaker community in which a basket, box, or cupboard originated. After the Civil War, it became difficult for the Shakers to compete with industrialization, the American desire for material goods, and an increasingly relaxed life-style. Between 1875 and 1900, more than a dozen Shaker communities closed. As the people moved, they took many of their furnishings to their new community or auctioned them. After fifty or one hundred years, it is incredibly difficult to sort out points of origin.

Many dealers insist that they be told the specific community in which a particular item was produced before they purchase it, so that they can pass on the information to the next buyer. In this way, supposition eventually is thought to be fact.

There are relatively few antiques dealers in the United States who specialize in Shaker, and seldom does a significant sewing cabinet or trestle table reach the market or auction block without their knowledge. The odds of a great Shaker treasure finding its way undiscovered to a mall show in Memphis or a shop in Seattle are slim.

The best guides for the casual collector are the books of John Kassay and Robert Meader. Also, make a periodic pilgrimage to one of the museums or restorations that feature Shaker items.

Furniture

The Shakers first began making furniture in the late eighteenth century. But, after the Civil War, the quality and quantity of furniture produced by the Shakers gradually diminished as membership in the sect fell. Communities closed, and Shakers moved to surviving settlements, bringing their furnishings with them. Because there was little work for Shaker carpenters, the level of craftsmanship declined over time.

Before the decline, white pine was used in much of the furniture produced by the Shakers. Maple, cherry, and walnut were used only on selected pieces. For example, maple was chosen for table legs, bedposts, and chairs. The Shakers finished their furniture with varnish, stain, or paint. Thinned paint or "wash" that allowed the natural grain of the wood to show through was also used.

It is difficult to accurately date Shaker furniture because the styles changed very little during most of the nineteenth century. Also, there was a significant amount of duplication from one community to another as settlements shared their furniture designs. Identification is further complicated by the fact that the Shaker craftsmen rarely signed their work.

Chairs

Other than footstools, Shaker chairs were about the only item sold to the outside world. The Shakers began selling chairs in the late 1780s, but it was not until the 1850s that they began to market the chairs in quantity.

In 1873, the Shakers built a chair factory and began to produce chairs in eight sizes. They were numbered 0 to 7 from smallest to largest. The number was impressed into the back of the top slat of most of the chairs.

The Shakers also put a gold decal or transfer on most of the rocking chairs made in their Mount Lebanon factory. A statement in an 1874 catalogue said, "Look for our trademark before purchasing — no chair is genuine without it. Our trademark is a gold transfer, and is designed to be ornamental."

The Shakers made chair seats from splint, rush, cane, leather (rarely), or worsted wool tapes known as "listing." As you look for Shaker chairs, don't be concerned if the tapes on a chair have been replaced, as this doesn't greatly affect the value. Usually, the transfer or decal will also be missing by the time a chair makes it to the auction house or antiques shop. The most important thing on a Shaker chair is the finish. The original finish is critical and the value will be diminished if the chair has been redone. Original production rocking chairs were dipped in vats of stain and will have a mahogany, ebony (black), or natural finish. The Shakers called the natural maple finish "white."

Interestingly, the Shakers used a form of division of labor to construct the chairs. They rotated jobs to combat boredom and were trained to complete different tasks. The sisters stained the chairs and taped the seats while the brothers turned out the parts and assembled the chairs. They operated their chair factory at Mount Lebanon until the late 1930s.

As you look for Shaker production rocking chairs, use the following information as a guide.

Size	Value	Comments
0 & 1	$850-1,350	Probably the most difficult two sizes to obtain.
2	$750-1,150	Also an uncommon size.
3 & 4	$550-675	The most common.
5	$850-1,000	Less common than 3 & 4.
6 & 7	$850-1,250	Certainly not rare, but the most practical and functional.

Note: The addition of a cushion rail to the top of a chair usually adds $75-125 to its value. If the chair still bears its transfer or decal, it may be worth an additional $35-45.

Other Shaker Collectibles

Shaker seed boxes have become highly collectible and hard to find. Originally, the Shakers took these boxes to general stores in the spring and left the seeds on consignment. They returned in the fall to pick up any extra packets or "papers" and the boxes. Then the boxes were cleaned, repainted, and re-labeled. An old Shaker seed box probably has a build-up of exterior labels. Check closely where the label is frayed or torn to see if another label is peeking through. Seldom is a perfect label found on an old box.

In the late 1970s, these boxes were priced in the $150-200 range, but they have increased significantly in price. It is essential that the label be at least eighty to ninety percent intact to have much value. Many of the boxes had interior labels on the lift lid in addition to the rectangular exterior label.

Shaker almanacs are also popular collectibles. The Shakers had the almanacs printed and then distributed them through many of the drug stores or general stores that sold the Shakers' products. The name of the individual distributor is usually found stamped on the back of each almanac. The books were handed out by the thousands in New England each year.

Auction Prices

The following information will give you an idea of the value of many different Shaker collectibles.

Portland, Maine
May 27, 1983
- Shaker sewing desk attributed to Elder Henry Green, $21,000
- Lady's cloak with hood, lining, and Sabbathday Lake label, $525
- Number 7 rocking chair from Mount Lebanon, $975
- Clothes brush from Alfred, $85
- Yellow painted miniature swift from Sabbathday Lake, $60
- Postcards sold by the Shakers at various communities showing scenes of their daily lives, $25 each

Kingston, Massachusetts
June 12, 1983
- Yellow 2 7/8″ oval box, $8,000
- Canterbury or Enfield, New Hampshire, sewing desk, $26,000
- Flax wheel signed S.R.A.L., Alfred, Maine, $412.50
- Tailoring counter, $2,860
- Small basket with slide lid, $181.50
- New Lebanon, New York, cobbler's bench, $3,630
- Number 6 slat-back armed rocking chair, Mount Lebanon, New York, $990
- "Goose" iron, $214.50
- Hanging wall sconce, $275

- Green 9″ oval box, $715
- Rug beater with partial Mount Lebanon label, $104.50
- Natural finish 12″ oval box, $247.50
- Refinished Mount Lebanon footstool with label, $275

For More Information

Unquestionably, the best source of information for potential collectors is a leisurely walk through a settlement restoration or a museum where Shaker furniture and other artifacts are on display. We have selected the five locations below based on personal experience. Each provides the visitor with an opportunity for a relaxed look at the past.
- Shelburne Museum, Shelburne, Vermont
- Hancock Shaker Community, Hancock, Massachusetts
- Shaker Museum, Old Chatham, New York
      Hancock and Old Chatham are in such close proximity that both could be visited in a single day.
- Shakertown at Pleasant Hill, Harrodsburg, Kentucky
- Golden Lamb Inn, Lebanon, Ohio
      The Golden Lamb is the oldest inn in Ohio and provides visitors with a great meal and lodging.
- Warren County Historical Society Museum, Lebanon, Ohio

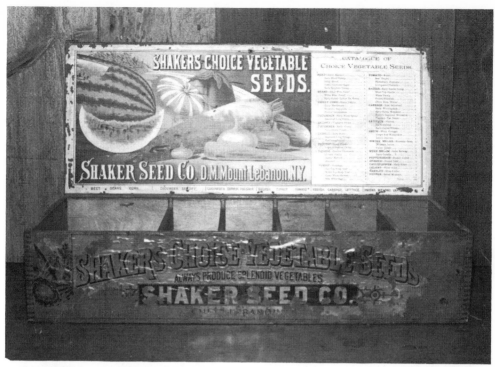

Rare seed box with colorful interior label
Mount Lebanon, New York, c. late nineteenth century. **$650-900**

Shaker brushes
New England, c. late nineteenth to early twentieth century. **$50-75**

Shaker seed boxes
Mount Lebanon, New York, c. 1860-1895.
$400-650

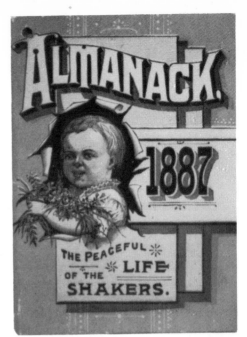

1887 Shaker Almanack   **$40-50**

Shaker brushes

Maple turned handles, sold to the "world" in Shaker shops in most New England communities, c. late nineteenth century.

$75-95 *each*

1885 Shaker Almanac and two sheet tin water dippers

Almanac   **$40-50**

Dippers   **$65-75** *each*

Shaker sewing boxes
Finger lap construction, wooden bail handle, New England, original varnished finish, c. late nineteenth century. **$175-200** each

Shaker pickle jar
Embossed, c. late nineteenth century. The Shakers purchased bottles from companies in the "world" and applied their own paper labels. **$100-125**

Shaker berry pail or miniature bucket
New England, staved construction with iron bands, c. late nineteenth century. **$175-250**

Shaker Extract of Roots bottle
Original paper label, c. late nineteenth century. **$95-125**

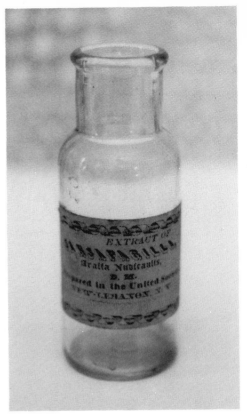

Shaker Horseradish bottle
Paper label, Portland, Maine, c. late nineteenth century. **$175-225**

Shaker Sarsaparilla bottle
New Lebanon, New York, paper label, c. 1860. **$115-130**

Shaker box or carrier
Pine, painted, possibly used in the seed industry, New England, mid-nineteenth century. **$400-500**

Shaker number 6 rocking chair and taped footstool
Mount Lebanon, New York, c. late nineteenth century.
Rocking chair: **$850-1,250**
Footstool (replaced tapes): **$95-125**

Shaker hair restorer bottle
Embossed lettering, c. late nineteenth century. **$55-75**

Shaker number 7 rocking chair
Cushion rail, Mount Lebanon, New York, c. late nineteenth century. **$1,200-1,400**

143

Shaker dining chair
Watervilet, New York, maple, original taped
seat, nineteenth century. **$1,000-1,250**

Shaker footstool
Original decal on the bottom of the stool,
Mount Lebanon, New York, c. late nineteenth
century. **$130-175**

Shaker rocking chair
Not made to sell to the "world," probably New
Lebanon, New York, c. early nineteenth
century. **$1,000-1,500**

144

Shaker desk
Black paint, pine, dovetailed top and pegged base, Harvard, Massachusetts, legs taper to less than ½" at base, lift lid, c. 1840.
$6,000-8,000

Shaker armchair
Replaced taped seat, probably from Ohio, c. mid-nineteenth century. $1,000-1,300

Shaker desk, interior view

Shaker ladder-back chairs
Painted, c. mid-nineteenth century. $650-750

6 Potpourri

This section includes the many types of country antiques that do not readily fall within a specific area. Trade signs, teddy bears, cast iron hitching posts, and cranberry scoops, all eagerly collected across the nation, fall into this category.

Teddy Bears

In the last few years, teddy bears have become highly desirable as collectibles. The American love for teddy bears all began November 15, 1902, when the *Washington Post* first linked a bear to Teddy Roosevelt. A reporter described how Roosevelt refused to kill a bear that had been captured for him. Clifford Berryman, a cartoonist with the *Washington Post,* probably began the national mania when his drawing of the event appeared in the November 16 edition of the paper.

A businessman in Brooklyn by the name of Morris Michtom saw the cartoon and had his wife Rose produce two bears for display in his store window. The demand for the bears became so great that the Michtoms formed the Ideal Novelty and Toy Company in 1907 to turn out thousands of the bears. The Steiff Company in Germany was making bears and other stuffed animals during approximately the same period. By 1907, the German firm was selling more than one million bears a year. Few of the Ideal or Steiff bears made before 1910 carry the company name.

The bears shown on the following pages are typically priced in the $120-350 range. Several years ago, these same bears could have been found for $15-45.

Display case for spools of thread
Used in general store, maple, refinished, c.
late nineteenth to early twentieth century.
$225-275

Shoe repair sign
Pine-framed tin sign, c. early twentieth
century. ***$75-110***

Sign from early 1890s resort
Pine. ***$175-200***

Coffee box
Frayed paper labels, pine, c. late nineteenth
to early twentieth century. ***$65-75*** *as is*
$150-175 *with original paper*
labels in good to excellent condition

Jewelry store advertising sign
C. 1870s.   **$300-385**

Soap box from general store
Used on counter for display, original condi-
tion, c. 1930.   **$60-70**

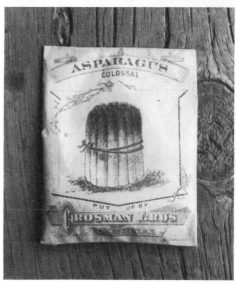

Hiram Sibley seed packets or "papers"
Original contents, c. 1890.   **$9-15** *each*

Counter display for seed packets or "papers"
Pine, c. 1900-1920. **$45-55**

Rooster weather vane
Copper, c. late nineteenth century. **$550-650**

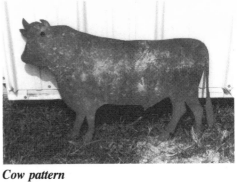

Cow pattern
Galvanized tin, 14″ × 30″, used by Minnesota blacksmith in making weather vanes, c. 1890 to early 1900s. **$225-250**

Horse weather vane pattern
C. 1890 to early 1900s. **$200-225**

Windmill weight
Cast iron, c. late nineteenth to early twentieth century. **$225-250**

Windmill weight
Cast iron, never painted, made by Hummer
Company of Elgin, Illinois, c. late nineteenth
century. $800-1,000

Windmill weight
Cast iron, painted, c. 1900. $650-800

Windmill weight
Cast iron, c. late nineteenth to early twentieth
century. $225-325

Windmill weight
Cast iron, two pieces bolted together, tail
broken off, c. late nineteenth century.
$300-350

Windmill weight
Cast iron, c. 1890-1900. **$750-800**

Windmill weight
Cast iron, c. late nineteenth century to early twentieth century. **$400-500**

Windmill weight
Cast iron, c. early nineteenth century.
$400-450

Rare sulky driver and horse weather vane
Copper, c. 1880. **$2,200-3,000**

Sheet-metal weather vane
Painted, c. 1900. The blacksmith weather vane patterns were used to trace the design on iron or sheet metal. **$200-225**

Prancing horse weather vane
Copper, c. late nineteenth century.

$1,000-1,200

Carrousel horse's head
Pine, c. early 1900s.

$250-300

Rocking horse
Original condition, c. late nineteenth century. This horse was carved from pine in several sections, then glued or bolted together. Stuffing was used to cover the horse, and a "skin" of heavy fabric was applied. Many of the horses have lost their stuffing and skin and have been refinished.

$600-750

Carrousel horse
Hand-carved pine, c. early 1900s.

$2,000-2,500

Rocking horse
Replaced tail, c. late nineteenth century.
$575-775

Rocking horse
Original condition, c. late nineteenth to early twentieth century.
$600-750

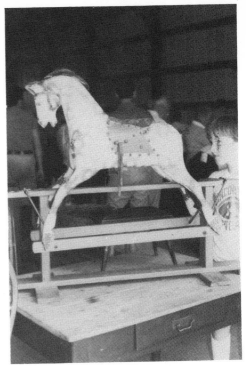

Rocking horse
Replaced saddle, painted, c. early twentieth century.
$500-600

Rocking horse
Painted pine, c. 1860-1880. The head and neck, legs, and body or trunk were made separately, then fitted together. Few of the horses were made from a single block of wood.
$500-600

Rocking horse
Mass-produced "Black Beauty," original painted condition, c. 1930-1940s. **$125-150**

154

Peddle-driven horse
Mass-produced, original painted condition, pine, c. 1930-1940s. **$75-85**

Horse pull toy (at right)
Horse-hair covering, pine base, c. early 1900s. **$135-150**

Electric horse machine
Original paint and plug, c. 1950. **$400-600**

Horse pull toy
Plaster of paris over wood frame, c. early 1900s. **$65-75**

Rocking horse
Platform style, plaster of paris over pine, original paint, c. 1900. **$500-575**

Child's push sleigh
Factory-made, c. late nineteenth century. **$250-350**

Noah's ark
Homemade version, painted, original condition, approximately 22″ × 20″, c. 1930s-1940s. **$375-450**

Checkerboard
Pine, painted, c. 1900. **$300-375**

Checkerboard
Painted, pine, uncommon style, c. mid-nineteenth century. **$500-600**

Checkerboards
Painted, pine, c. late nineteenth to early twentieth century. $275-325 each

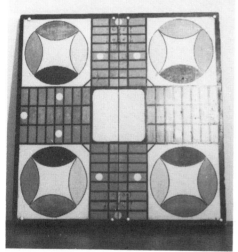

Parchesi board
New England, c. 1900. $450-500

Cast iron hitching post
Painted, c. late nineteenth century. These have been reproduced in quantity for the past thirty years. The older versions have more carefully detailed features on the man's face and should show signs of weather-related wear. $300-500

157

Decoy
Carved by G. Wright Gregan, northern New
Brunswick, Canada, c. 1900-1910. **$300-400**

Folk art carved moose
Light green wash, Maine, c. 1900. A "wash"
is a thinned or watered down paint that is
lightly brushed over an object and allows the
natural grain of the wood to show through.
$350-450

**Pair of red-breasted merganser working
decoys**
New England, c. 1910. A "working" decoy
was designed to be used, not for display.
$1,000-1,300 for the pair

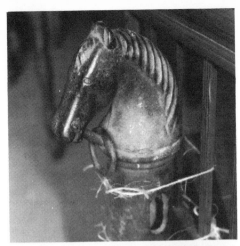

Cast iron hitching post
Original iron pole, never painted, c. 1880.
$350-400

Carved bust
Pine, unfinished.   *$200-300*

"Grotesque" jug
Contemporary folk art.   *$95-135*

Child's wagon
Pine, painted red, c. early 1900s.   *$250-325*

Wicker rocking chair
Painted white, c. 1930.   *$175-200*

Child's wagon
Pine, painted, iron wheels, c. early 1900s.
                    $200-300

Farm wagon
Used for a variety of tasks, original condition,
pine, c. 1920.   *$400-600*

Wheelbarrow
Painted pine, c. early twentieth century.
$125-175

Parade torch
Tin, c. 1870-1880.　　　　　　　　**$50-60**

Barn lantern
Pine, painted blue, replaced glass, found in eastern Massachusetts, c. late nineteenth century.　　**$200-275**

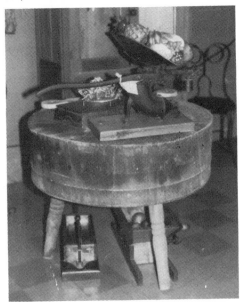

Chopping or meat block
Maple, made from a section of tree, turned legs, painted, c. early 1900s.　　**$375-450**

Nest of grain measures
Factory-made, c. early twentieth century.
$100-130 *for the nest of five*

Carpenter's tool box
Pine, nailed corners, refinished, c. 1880.
$65-75

Coffee mill
Used on store counter, Elgin, Illinois, National Mill, eagle finial, original paint and decorative decals, c. late nineteenth century.
$500-675

Sausage bench and grinder
Painted, c. late nineteenth to early twentieth century.

Bench:	**$55-65**
Cast iron sausage grinder:	**$38-45**
Bench and attached grinder:	**$75-110**

Keg or small barrel with spigot
Staved and bound with iron bands, c. 1890.
$50-60

String holders
Turned wood and cast iron, c. late nineteenth century.
Turned wooden string holder (left): **$135-145**
Cast iron string holder (right): **$55-65**

Cranberry scoop
Sheet metal, c. late nineteenth century.
$30-35

Foot warmer
Pierced tin, pine frame, possibly from Pennsylvania, bail handle for carrying, c. mid-nineteenth century. **$100-115**

Fireplace bellows
Mid-nineteenth century.   **$65-75**

Yarn winder
Pine, mortise and tenon construction, c. mid-nineteenth century.   **$115-125**

Staved flour barrel
Iron bands with wooden replacement bands at bottom, weathered condition, c. early twentieth century.   **$45-55**

Spinning wheel
Maple, refinished, c. 1840-1860.   **$140-160**

163

Table loom
Pine, never painted, c. mid-nineteenth century. **$200-225**

Printer's type
Used for printing banners and posters, c. late nineteenth century. **$2-3** a letter
Type box: **$15-18**

Copper wash boiler with original lid
Burnished, c. early twentieth century. **$50-55**

Fire bucket
Galvanized metal, often filled with sand to put out fires, painted, c. early twentieth century. **$25-30**

Copper tea kettle
Originally nickel plated, bail handle, factory-made, c. first quarter of the twentieth century. **$55-65**

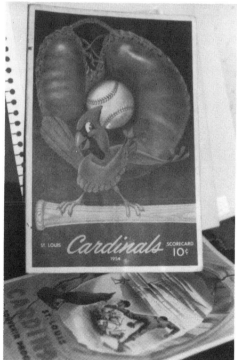

Locomotive oil can
Brass, c. 1920. **$25-35**

Baseball scorecards
1949 and 1954 St. Louis Cardinals, excellent condition. **$12** *each*

Brass candlesticks
English, c. nineteenth century.
$100-300 *each*

Copper wash boiler
Sawbuck stand, c. early twentieth century.
Wash boiler:	**$50-55**
Stand:	**$25-35**
Boiler and stand:	**$100-110**

Child's ice cream chair and table set
C. 1920.   **$325-500**

Children's shoe molds
Maple, various sizes, used in late nineteenth-century New England shoe factories.
                              $3-5 each

Child's wood-burning stove and accessories
Cast iron, c. early 1900s.   **$300-450**

Child's stove and cooking utensils
Cast iron, c. late nineteenth century.

$375-450

Wicker baby carriage
C. 1910. $175-225

Black doll
C. late nineteenth to early twentieth century.

$300-325

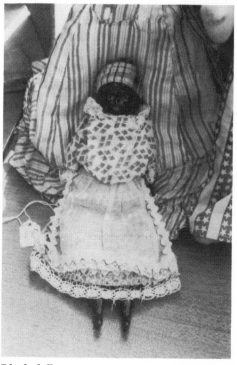

Black doll
C. late nineteenth century. $300-400

167

China dolls
C. early twentieth century.   **$150-225**

Nineteenth-century doll
New England.   **$275-325**

Black "bottle" doll
C. early twentieth century.   **$75-95**

Black doll
C. 1900.   **$75-100**

Cloth doll
C. nineteenth century.   **$375-450**

Cloth doll
C. nineteenth century.   **$375-450**

Cloth doll
C. nineteenth century.   **$275-325**

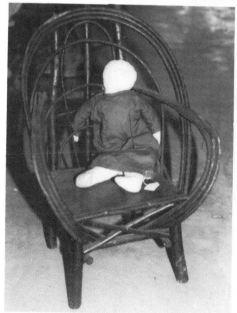

Newly made Amish doll   **$30-50**

Child's rustic twig chair
Painted, c. 1900.   **$100-125**

169

Patriotic hooked rug
C. 1940.   *$300-400*

Stuffed rabbit
C. 1940.   *$55-65*

Heart hooked rug
24" × 36", c. 1930.   *$200-275*

Stuffed monkey
C. 1950.   *$20-25 each*

Double wedding ring hooked rug
Hooked in Indiana, 3' × 3', c. 1890-1900.
                                          $300-400

Winter scene hooked rug
C. 1930. **$125-175**

Coverlet
C. 1840. **$800-1,200**

Schoolhouse quilt
C. mid-nineteenth century. **$1,200-1,500**

Coverlet
Ohio, c. 1830-1850. **$350-500**

Final Examination

This is, hopefully, the most difficult test we have devised. We have spent literally an hour thinking of questions that will cause massive anxiety attacks when you realize that you did not adequately prepare. Please do not embarrass us and yourself with a poor performance on the test. We have been friends too long.

Directions
1. Read each question carefully.
2. Don't write in the book.
3. Keep your eyes on your own book.
4. Select the best (usually) answer.
5. Don't ask your neighbor for help.

1. This is a piece of _____ pottery.
   a. stoneware
   b. redware
   c. the terms are interchangeable

2. It could also be described as
   a. molded rather than thrown
   b. thrown rather than molded
   c. ovoid
   d. b and c are both correct

3. (True) (False) Stenciled stoneware is usually older than stoneware decorated with a brush or slip cup.

4. The shape of this stoneware piece suggests that it dates from
   a. before 1850
   b. about 1860
   c. about 1880
   d. impossible to tell from the jug's shape

5. Which of the pottery marks below would make it an *especially* good piece?
   a. Red Wing Stoneware Co.
   b. Julius Norton, Bennington, Vermont
   c. Peoria Pottery Co.
   d. Hamilton & Jones, Greensboro, Pennsylvania

6. (True) (False) This is a Boston rocker.
7. The approximate value of this chair is
   a. less than $125
   b. more than $200 but less than $400
   c. more than $400 but less than $650
   d. more than $700
8. The stretchers and the legs of this chair are made of
   a. oak
   b. pine
   c. walnut
   d. maple
9. The seat is made of
   a. oak
   b. pine
   c. walnut
   d. maple

10. (True) (False) The corner cupboard dates from before 1870.
11. The cupboard has sixteen panes of glass, or "_____."
12. Which of the colors listed below would add the most value to the cupboard?
   a. red
   b. green
   c. blue
   d. white
13. What is the approximate value of the cupboard with its original paint?
   a. $400-600
   b. $700-900
   c. more than $1,000

14. This candle mold is made of
    a. pewter
    b. tin
    c. zinc
    d. none of the above
15. Another name for a nineteenth-century traveling candle maker was a _____.
16. (True) (False) This candle mold dates from the late eighteenth century.
17. What is the approximate value of this sixty-tube candle mold?
    a. $75
    b. $100
    c. $150
    d. more than $275

18. This type of chair is named for
    a. Marie Windsor
    b. Duke Windsor
    c. Harry Windsor
    d. none of the above
19. The legs of this chair are
    a. splayed
    b. dovetailed to the plank seat
    c. pinned to the seat
    d. none of the above
20. This type of chair is called a
    a. fan-back
    b. comb-back
    c. bow-back
    d. none of the above

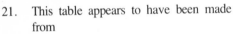

21. This table appears to have been made from
    a. oak
    b. pine
    c. walnut
    d. maple

22. The table dates from *approximately*
    a. 1800
    b. 1820
    c. 1840
    d. 1860

23. (True) (False) The porcelain drawer pulls appear to be replacements.

24. The refinished bedside table is worth about
    a. $100
    b. $250-275
    c. more than $400
    d. less than $100

25. A "chicken pecking corn" stoneware crock in excellent condition from Fort Edward, New York, is worth about
    a. $100-200
    b. $225-375
    c. $450-550
    d. more than $1,000

26. How would you date this crock?
    a. 1820-1840
    b. 1850-1860
    c. 1870s
    d. 1890s

27. (True) (False) The crock would be even more valuable if the chicken were pecking to his left rather than to his right.

28. The woodenware in this bowl is made of
    a. oak
    b. pine
    c. walnut
    d. maple
29. (True) (False) All of these implements appear to have been factory made.
30. The implements date from _____ 1880.
    a. before
    b. after

31. The founder of the Shaker movement in America was
    a. Sara Lee
    b. Bruce Lee
    c. Brenda Lee
    d. Ann Lee
32. A Shaker seed box with an exterior label in good condition is worth
    a. $75-125
    b. $130-200
    c. $210-300
    d. more than $300
33. These Shaker seed boxes date from about
    a. 1790-1830
    b. 1840-1870
    c. 1880-1890
    d. 1930-1950

34. The Hart's Seed boxes are worth about
    a. $40-70 each
    b. $100-150 each
    c. more than $150 each
    d. less than $20 each

35. The Shakers made rocking chairs for the "world" in _____ sizes.

36. (True) (False) If a rocking chair has a taped seat, it is probably Shaker.

37. This stoneware pitcher was
    a. thrown on a potter's wheel
    b. molded rather than thrown

38. The cobalt decoration was applied with a
    a. sponge
    b. slip cup
    c. brush
    d. none of the above

39. Most country baskets are made from
    a. willow splint
    b. oak splint
    c. ash splint
    d. wicker splint
    e. b and c are used equally
    f. a and c are used equally

40. (True) (False) This basket would be less valuable if it were painted.

41. (True) (False) A swing-handle basket usually is more valuable than a similar basket with a fixed handle.

42. (True) (False) This basket, in good condition, is worth more than $200.

43. This country dry sink is probably made from
    a. oak
    b. pine
    c. walnut
    d. maple

44. If the sink was made between 1840 and 1860, it probably was not made from
   a. oak
   b. pine
   c. walnut
   d. maple
45. The sink is worth approximately
   a. $250-350
   b. $400-600
   c. $800-1,000
   d. $1,200-1,400

Matching
46. _____ Wallace Nutting
47. _____ Kutztown, Pennsylvania
48. _____ Sam Pennington
49. _____ Shelburne, Vermont
50. _____ Alan I. Weintraub
   a. the editor of the *Maine Antiques Digest*
   b. the location of one of the nation's great displays of country antiques
   c. an early twentieth-century manufacturer of reproduction American furniture
   d. the location of an annual folk art festival
   e. one of the nation's leading authorities on antiques

Bonus Question
Worth Three Points
This solitary soldier is the unknown collector. He represents all of us who have gone after him and suffered from overexposure to under-cooked hot dogs, Pepsi without fizz, and the "home-baked" apple pie from the little church on the corner that was made for the Easter brunch and sold to us in August.

Who is this man?
   a. Brom Bones
   b. Larry Vail
   c. Don Brown
   d. Bobby Farling
   e. Dale Troyer
   f. all of the above

Answers

1. a
2. b
3. false
4. a
5. b
6. false — This is a Salem rocker. A Boston rocker has a rolling or scrolled seat, not a flat seat.
7. b
8. d
9. b
10. true
11. lights
12. c
13. c
14. b
15. chandler
16. false — Mid-nineteenth century is closer.
17. d
18. d
19. a
20. c
21. b
22. d
23. true
24. b
25. c
26. c
27. true
28. d
29. true
30. b
31. d
32. d
33. c
34. a
35. eight
36. false
37. b
38. a
39. e
40. false
41. true
42. true
43. b
44. a
45. b
46. c
47. d
48. a
49. b
50. e

Bonus Question

The best answer is probably f. If you were close, give yourself three points credit.

Scoring Scale

	Number Correct
You should put together your own slide show and go on the road with it. You are truly a national authority.	44-50
You probably have a friend who is a national authority. The next time you take the test, sit closer to him.	38-43
Your performance could best be described as mediocre.	32-37
You did not do well. If the American Carnival Glass Association is meeting near your home, you might want to attend.	24-31

Bibliography

Gould, Mary Earle. *Early American Wooden-ware*. Charles E. Tuttle, 1962.

Greer, Georgeanna. *American Stoneware, the Art and Craft of Utilitarian Potters*. Shiffer, 1981.

Guilland, Harold. *Early American Folk Pottery*. Chilton, 1971.

Kassay, John. *The Book of Shaker Furniture*. University of Massachusetts Press, 1980.

Kauffman, Henry. *Pennsylvania Dutch American Folk Art*. Dover, 1964.

Klamkin, Marian. *Hands to Work: Shaker Folk Art and Industries*. Dodd, Mead, and Company, 1972.

Larason, Lew. *The Basket Collector's Book*. Science Press.

Little, Nina Fletcher. *Neat and Tidy*. E. P. Dutton, 1980.

Meader, Robert. *Illustrated Guide to Shaker Furniture*. Dover, 1972.

Osgood, Cornelius. *The Jug and Related Stoneware of Bennington*. Charles E. Tuttle, 1971.

Raycraft, Don and Carol. *The Basket Book*. Collector Books, 1981.

———. *Collector's Guide to Kitchen Antiques*. Collector Books, 1980.

———. *Country Baskets*. Wallace-Homestead, 1977.

———. *Shaker — A Collector's Source Book*. Wallace-Homestead, 1980.

Teleki, Gloria. *The Baskets of Rural America*. E. P. Dutton, 1975.

———. *Collecting Traditional American Baskets*. E. P. Dutton, 1975.

Webster, Donald Blake. *Decorated Stoneware of North America*. Charles E. Tuttle, 1971.

About the Authors

Don and Carol Raycraft, authors of thirteen books on country antiques, live with their three sons on a four generation farm near Normal, Illinois. They live in a mid-19th century barn which is charmingly decorated and furnished in Shaker and American country antiques. Both attended Illinois State University where she received a bachelor's degree in elementary education and her husband earned a bachelor's, master's and doctoral degrees in education and psychology.